To Chester County and
those who care for its preservation

CHESTER COUNTY

a photographic journey

Special thanks to Maxim Dadoun, Frederick Miller, and Ben Pearce.

Published in 1997
Printed in Korea

Library of Congress Catalog Number 97-26070
ISBN: 0-89802-692-X
First Edition, August, 1997
Second Edition, November, 2006

PHOTOGRAPHY: Mike Biggs
TEXT: Catherine Quillman
DESIGN DIRECTION: B. Ben Pearce
PUBLISHER: Maxim Dadoun/Frederick Miller
PRODUCTION: Pat Young

CHESTER COUNTY
a photographic journey

Photography by Mike Biggs/Text by Catherine Quillman

Designed by Bernard Ben Pearce

PUBLISHED BY THE JARED COMPANY/MILLER PUBLISHING, INC.
WILMINGTON, DELAWARE

This book was made possible through the generosity and help of the following:

Chester County Economic Development Council

Cephalon

Brandywine River Museum

Immaculata University

RE/MAX Professional Realty, Inc.

Willow Financial Bank

Genesis HealthCare

MEDecision

Wilkinson Builders

Devon Horse Show & Country Fair

Waterloo Gardens

Morris Capital Advisors, Inc.

Bernardon Haber Holloway Architects PC

The Hankin Group

Vanguard

Jackson Cross Partners

Longwood Gardens

Chester County Historical Society

contents

the beginnings

The Beginnings

Like many unusual stories, the history of this region west of Philadelphia begins with a gift. In 1680, an English Quaker named William Penn received the land as part of a vast territory given by King Charles II who named him sole proprietor to cover a debt of 16,000 pounds owed to Penn's late father, a prominent admiral. Although the Dutch and Swedes had occupied part of the region for nearly forty years, Penn knew it only as lying somewhere north of the "Great Bay," between the fortieth and forty-third parallels. As interior land, not close to any large body of water, Penn's land, or Pennsylvania as it was soon called, had only recently been claimed by the English, who as early as 1664 had seized lands from the Dutch that would become New York, New Jersey, and Delaware.

Chester County became one of three counties Penn established in 1682, the year he sailed up the Delaware River and landed at the Dutch settlement of Upland, now Chester, Pennsylvania. Until Lancaster County was formed in 1729, Chester County extended west almost to the Blue Ridge Mountains and south into present-day Delaware County.

History books generally make much of the fact that Penn knew very little about his new colony and put his faith in the Indians by negotiating a purchase price in a treaty vowing to take only as much land that a man could walk in three days. Like many of Penn's treaties, the so-called "Walking Purchase" cannot be fully documented, but it does suggest the arbitrary manner in which boundaries were then determined. Indeed, Penn would later become embroiled in political and financial battles that kept him away from his new colony for all but three short visits and even landed him in debtor's prison. Still, almost from the moment Penn and his fellow Quakers stepped ashore from their sailing vessel, the Welcome, they knew that the King had granted them a bargain.

In his promotional reports to the Free Society of Traders in London, Penn found no need to exaggerate the new colony's natural abundance. He described the land as rich and wondrous, a place so sheltered by a series of mountains that its valleys formed a sun-filled plain and a "fat, fast land." Geographically, Chester County's location was ideal. There were natural springs and streams here, and its location on the Atlantic slope between a wide swath of tidewater marshland and a range of mountains created a mild climate—Penn compared it to that of Naples, Italy and the south of France. These were important factors in the new colony's long range economic success. The inclination sent waterpower hurtling downstream and made it easier for the colonists to establish Pennsylvania's first mills and other water-powered industries. Typically, a number of enterprises were powered by a single stream. The Brandywine alone, which descends for about fifty miles from its source near Honey Brook, would eventually power one-hundred fifty mills, including jointly-operated grist and lumber mills and water-powered industries that made cider, hemp, flax oil, snuff, paper, textiles, and even gunpowder and iron products. The countryside was also rich in mineral and alluvial deposits such as kaolin and red clay which enabled the colonists to make both pottery and fine china. There were also large deposits of limestone which, like red clay, had a dual purpose: processed in lime kilns, the stone was initially used to make a type of mortar and later as a soil fertilizer (perhaps the single most important discovery made in the early 1800s). Within a short time, sturdy brick and fieldstone structures replaced the scattered log cabins, lean-tos and early caves of the Dutch and Swedes and gave a sense of permanence to the region.

Chester County was also close to the new city of Philadelphia and the center of a network of old Indian trails that extended westward to the important trading outposts of Lancaster and Harrisburg, then known as Paxtang. Aside from giving the county a distinctive destiny and character, with taverns cropping up on every corner and packs of drovers herding cows, pigs, and even turkeys down the dusty roads, the proximity of the city influenced local tastes in everything from architecture and the decorative arts to the customs of country living. There were even early Philadelphians who regarded Chester County as an ideal spot for a second home, or country seat, as they were called.

With such a setting, it's perhaps no surprise that even in the midst of William Penn's first winter, he remained optimistic about his new colony's potential. Writing to a friend in England on December 29, 1682, Penn is particularly quaint in his enthusiasm for the "outward things"— the "plentiful" springs and the "natural produce." He observed that the county's "mixture of meadow, wood and hills, [gave] it a pleasant appearance" and that the wild turkeys weighed forty to fifty pounds and the deer were "bigger than ours." All served to create a restful and peaceful atmosphere, he exclaimed in summary, "freed from the anxious and troublesome solicitations, hurries, and perplexities of woeful Europe!"

In 1684, the discovery of iron ore in Chester County confirmed Penn's faith; indeed, he rightly considered it to be the colony's most important asset and his greatest stroke of luck. Of course, like many windfalls, its existence had long been known by the Indians. Legend has it, that an Indian squaw blithely led Samuel Nutt, an English Quaker, to a large outcropping of iron ore near the present-day village of Warwick. Thanks to an unusual geological fault, the ore literally rested on the surface of the earth and was easily mined. By the late 1700s and the American Revolution, Warwick had become the center of the colonial iron industry. With so much to gain, it was a wonder that Penn even had to promote his colony as the site of the great "Holy Experiment," where people of different faiths and backgrounds could live harmoniously. Although Penn's experience as a trustee of a Quaker community in West New Jersey certainly influenced his vision, he may have indirectly undertaken the greatest marketing scheme in opening the doors to the persecuted and besieged. With King Charles II newly restored to the throne and England seeing better times, even the Quakers, who were largely middle-class and educated, must have had doubts about pulling up stakes and crossing the Atlantic for an unknown territory and fate. It was perhaps fortunate that the people Penn would address in a letter that preceded him as the "Inhabitants of Pennsylvania" were also a gentle people.

The Swedes, in particular, were a harmonious presence. Although some were traders, many seemed to model their peaceful lifestyle after the Lenni Lenape Indians, a group Penn later described as being "never in haste, for they are everywhere at home." In contrast with the Dutch who laid claim to the region through Henry Hudson's expedition of 1609, the Swedes based their land rights on outright purchase from the Indians. Their early accounts of life along the sandy banks of the Delaware River and further inland along the meadows of the Schuylkill basin read like fairy tales. When a boat approached the shore of a creek, or "kill," flocks of white cranes or swans rose into the air like enormous clouds and fish would practically leap into one's hands. Early paintings depict shorelines dotted with white-washed cabins, and squares of turned soil or tidy orchards that peeked through the dense trees and gave the landscape a cheerful, inviting appearance. As one Englishman observed, the Swedes lived "the easy life," content to "plant a little tobacco and a little Indian corn."

In his now famous letter, Penn assured these inhabitants that they would live by laws of their own making and that he only had improvements in store. In fact, with the exception of changing Upland's name to Chester (after Cheshire, England), the transfer of power was remarkably smooth for that era of feuds and conquest. Penn not only retained the Court at Upland, but allowed several Swedish officials to remain as members and to oversee the building of "mills, and the laying out of roads and bridle paths," as early agenda items were described.

The writings of Thomas Paschall, an Englishman who resided in Chester County in 1683, suggests that the Swedes and Dutch had little lasting influence, however. He writes that their authority was soon mitigated by the "throngs" of English settlers who arrived on Penn's heels. Those who obtained Penn grants—the aptly named "Adventurers"—faced a sprawling territory laced with Indian paths, deep streams and steep hills. But there were also many settlers who found it easier to purchase land directly from the Swedes. Thomas Paschall reported that they were willing to give up their land and homesteads for "almost nothing," citing as an example one property "worth at least three hundred pounds" was exchanged for a "cow, a sow and one hundred pumpkins."

In time, Chester County was not only settled by Quakers from England and Wales, but also the Welsh Baptists, French Catholics, German Lutherans, Scotch and Irish Presbyterians, and even a small Swiss faction called the Mennonites and the Amish. Gradually, the Dutch, Swedes, and Indians disappeared from the landscape, leaving behind only such customs as planting corn, maintaining orchards and allowing their cows and other livestock to roam free. Yet by the late 1700s, no other colony but Pennsylvania had such a mixture of religions, languages, and nationalities.

The authors of *A History of Chester County* (1881), J. Smith Futhey and Gilbert Cape, note that Pennsylvania had no central land office until 1729, and that consequently, "settlers were generally allowed to take up lands where they pleased...." Land investment groups such as the West New Jersey Society also obtained large tracts of land, offering settlers the option of lease or purchase. With each new wave of immigrants, a pattern began to emerge: different groups tended to settle specific parts of the county, finding ways to make it hospitable and home-like. Chester County became a place where the people shaped the land as much as the land shaped the people.

The English Quakers who followed in Penn's footsteps, for instance, naturally had to produce what was most needed, but many were also experienced millwrights or were skilled in iron production. The Welsh, on the other hand, arriving from their homeland of craggy mountains and steep valleys, were well suited to the job of carving an early road system through the so-called "Welsh tract," which roughly extended along the eastern section of the Allegheny Path, from Upper Merion to present-day Downingtown. After failing to establish a barony there, the Welsh resettled in the northern part of the county, in townships such as Uwchlan and the Nantmeals. Their history can be traced today in villages and townships that retain their Welsh names, both in the northern region and the "Main Line," the region named after a rail spur of the Pennsylvania Railroad.

The typical pattern of settlement, clustering villages around a mill or along major crossroads, and to some extent even the Indians' skill in developing dry, level and direct paths, helped to create a Chester County that was beautiful in its randomness and orderliness. In the northwestern areas of the county, the landscape is still dotted with the small stone dwellings of the former miners, wood-cutters, and furnace workers who were recruited from Ireland and northern England to work in the region's iron industry.

The German migration of 1709 brought a group known as the Pietists whose beliefs, similar to the Quakers, were formed during the Protestant Reformation. They included the Swiss-born Amish and Mennonites, the Lutherans and the Rhineland Germans from the Rhine River Valley who were later called the Pennsylvania Dutch. The land they settled seemed perfectly suited to their needs. They knew how to manage waterpower and small hillside farms, and even the hard red soil of the region was similar to what they knew in their homeland. Like the English, they built spacious stone barns sheltered against a hillside.

After the Welsh, the second largest group to arrive on the shores of Delaware was the Scots and Scotch-Irish, a group so named because they had initially left their homeland for Ireland, which suffered hardships in 1699 and again after the potato famine of 1846. Those who arrived during the second wave of immigration generally took up lands further north in Chester County, in the Nantmeals and outlying townships such Wallace and West Caln, a place early township petitioners complained of being remote and "situate on the backside of a mountain." Today, the region's tall-steepled churches, one-room schools, and company towns, first built around early textile industries, attest to the long-staying power of the Scots and Scotch-Irish. Indeed, nearly everywhere in Chester County, the past is still visible in the landscape. As the pictorial journey of this book reveals, the King's grant was truly a remarkable gift.

The Downingtown log house is considered a marvel of Swedish-style log construction. Its restorers think it may have once served as a trading post since it was built on land bordering an Indian trail that was acquired by a French trader and merchant in 1703.

The steeply pitched roof (once covered with clay tiles) and small windows give this early stone home known as the "Beehive" in Thornbury Township a Dutch-style appearance. However, it was actually built around 1705 by an English family, the Woodwards, who had prospered as farmers within a few years of obtaining a Penn grant. All the activity here supposedly gave the home its name.

In planning his new colony, William Penn had envisioned a close-knit pattern of settlements in which the colonists might follow the European practice of living in villages or "greene countrie" towns like Philadelphia close to the countryside. In Chester County, people tended to live independently on farms eked out of the wilderness where they worked for generations.

The circa 1704 Brinton House in Dilworthtown evokes the rural simplicity of early Quaker life. Like the Beehive, it is built of stone cut to resemble bricks. Below, the Barnes-Brinton House in Chadds Ford.

Owned by the same family for generations, the Pennock House in London Grove is one of the few notable examples of a substantial colonial brick home.

The three-room, "Quaker plan" homes of the 1680s to the 1750s were often enlarged to include a wide central hall and an adjoining kitchen. Such improvements were usually not a case of keeping up with the Joneses, however. The Pennock House, for instance, evolved during two distinct periods of agriculture development, from 1750 to 1760 and 1800 to 1812.

Although the Quakers stressed modesty and restraint, the number of elegant details found in prosperous households is in keeping with their reputation for liberal hospitality and, hence, love of refinements.

Primitive Hall in nearby Chatham was built in 1738 in the latest Flemish-bond brick style. Some of its windows contain as many as thirty panes—a definite sign of affluence in colonial America. Below, its elegantly paneled corner fireplace.

This massive stone barn in East Bradford has unusual arched bays and an additional upper floor, a feature of a once common type of bank barn known as the "double decker."

The bank barn—so named because it was built into the bank of a hill—is also attributed to the area's Quakers. Sheltered from winds and weather, the bank barn enabled a farmer to drive a wagon into the upper level and toss hay into the loft or pour grain down chutes to the stalls below.

The array of 19th-century frame outbuildings of the Allerton farm near West Chester documents its years when it was famous for its "modern" dairying techniques.

Farmsteads throughout Chester County are fascinating visual documents of the agricultural boom years of 1800 to 1850 which were brought about by the enterprising and scientifically-minded Quaker farmers. With an eye towards improving dairy and crop production, they patented hundreds of new types of farm equipment—among them, hay mowers, grain drills and threshers.

The bank barn of nearby Lucky Hill Farm is in perfect harmony with the gentle slope of a hillside.

The Anselma mill, also known as the Collins mill, was built in 1747 by Samuel Lightfoot, then the township's largest taxpayer and the largest landholder with more than four-hundred acres in his name.

Although water-powered industries were part of his agenda, William Penn probably didn't anticipate the kind of settlements that sprang up around mill complexes here. In West Pikeland Township, for instance, the Lightfoot mill, later known as the Anselma and Collins mill, served both as a custom and merchant mill where corn and wheat were ground for farmers near and far. By the 1800s, the mill complex encompassed a busy railway station, a cooperative creamery, a one-room school, a coal and lumber yard and a general store (where the township's first telephone reportedly was installed).

Today, visitors come to its secluded location along Route 401 to see what has been called a rare document of early mill technology. Never updated, the mill still has its original wooden gearing and unusual decorative touches such as carved newel posts and scalloped grain chute ends.

The old miller's house and barn at nearby Pine Creek Mills, once a jointly-operated grist and lumber mill complex dating to 1795. Part of its machinery is now in the Smithsonian Institution.

An ornate wood "piazza" connects a building that has long housed the Inn at Historic Yellow Springs to the Lincoln Building, built around 1823.

The gentle shade gardens and wetlands that surround the Jenny Lind Spring House recreate the romantic setting once used by painters from the Pennsylvania Academy of the Fine Arts.

Once known as Bath, the village of Yellow Springs takes its name from the natural sulphur springs—there were also magnesium and iron springs—that trickle into the various baths and spring houses on the property. An 1814 advertisement proclaimed the waters as "unrivaled in the cure of chronic disease." The village was also the site of a Revolutionary War hospital, a state-run orphanage for the children of Civil War veterans, and a renowned school for landscape painters in the early 1900s.

The Marshalton Inn, pictured here with its former livery stable, was a drovers' stop throughout the 1800s. The village was named after Humphrey Marshall, a colonial scholar and agronomist who published America's first work on botany in 1785.

One of many historic districts in Chester County, Marshallton in West Bradford is a quintessential village, bisected by an old road and lined with a mix of 19th-century frame and brick homes. Many housed former general stores, cigar "factories," tinsmithing shops, oyster bars, millinery shops and other once essential enterprises. The village still has its network of backyard alleys, once used by shopkeepers and tradesmen.

Another Marshallton landmark: Its former blacksmith shop, in use until the 1940s.

This beautifully restored 18th-century home is located in the historic district of Wagontown. Farmers in the 19th century routinely covered stonework with plaster and whitewash, but today's homeowner generally prefers to show-off its timeless beauty.

◄ The Forks of the Brandywine, built in 1876, has a commanding view of West Brandywine Township where many Scots and Scotch-Irish settled among the hills and hollows of the countryside.

Simple, unadorned headstones line the cemetery at Birmingham Friends Meeting. A common grave for both British and American soldiers is believed to be located here.

During the American Revolution, on September 11, 1777, a burst of activity disrupted the serene setting of the Birmingham Friends Meeting. First, Continental soldiers took over the building for use as a hospital, displacing the Friends from their meeting. Later, the British invaded the site.

Although the Friends initially gathered for worship under a nearby sheltering tree, they were eventually forced to flee to nearby Sconneltown where they settled in a wheelwright shop. Its windows overlooked the advancing British troops, their uniforms creating a sea of scarlet through the valley.

Not unlike the covered bridges here, the county's distinctive 19th-century octagonal school houses rarely escape notice. This one stands on the grounds of Birmingham Friends.

The simple dome and clock tower of the Chester County Courthouse rises above the center of the borough. It was designed by Thomas U. Walter, who later went on to be the architect of the United States Capitol, among other government buildings.

For a few heady hours in April 1785, a settlement known as Turk's Head was the dramatic scene of a near riot between two reactionary groups—newspapers of the day called them the "Removalists" and "Anti-removalists"—who took opposite stands on a state law granting the removal of the county seat from the city of Chester, then part of Chester County.

The two groups fortified themselves with whiskey and grog and, carrying rifles and a small field cannon, had their last stand in front of the half-completed court house and jail then being built. Although the Removalists reportedly walked from Chester, the sincerity of both groups was questionable—the instigators were tavern owners who presumably had their own reasons for keeping commerce in their towns. In the end, the Removalists won without a shot fired, and the county seat was relocated at Turk's Head, west of Chester. The community is known today, of course, as West Chester.

The old library at West Chester University, a campus landmark for its locally-quarried "Brinton" serpentine. Below, an example of the beautiful iron ornamentation found in the borough.

MUS EUM
SH OP

CHESTER
COUNTY
HISTORICAL
SOCIETY

The arched entrance of a building long associated with the "collective memory" of Chester County—the Chester County Historical Society. Originally built for a horticultural society, the building is most famous as the site of anti-slavery meetings and the first Pennsylvania women's rights convention in 1852. It was designed in 1848 by Thomas U. Walter, the architect of the United States Capitol.

◀ The History Center of the Chester County Historical Society. The center was created when the society expanded into the adjacent colonial-revival style building—a former YMCA—on North High Street.

A display room of American Queen Anne furniture found at the historical society. The inlaid spice box (c.1740-1760) at the left is especially characteristic of the region.

Chester County was never a Dickensian vision of smoke stacks or sooty factories. And yet in the 1800s the term, "Made in Chester County," applied to an extraordinary diverse number of items, from blue jeans, iron stoves and wallpaper to hardwood furniture, clock cases and pottery. Examples are found in the Chester County Historical Society, which since its founding in 1893, has amassed a collection of some 50,000 objects and artifacts documenting nearly every aspect of the county's history.

A stately row of tall-case clocks. Most were made from imported English brass works and assembled in locally-made cabinets. Below, a display of redware pottery, named for its iron-rich clay.

A close-up of the stargazers stone reveals that it actually is composed of several pieces of quartz.

The stargazer's stone, which lies in an open field along Route 162 near Embreeville, is one of Chester County's curious and obscure landmarks. It marks the precise starting point of a survey made in 1764 by two surveyors, Charles Mason and Jeremiah Dixon, who were summoned from England to settle a boundary dispute between heirs of William Penn and the Calverts of Baltimore. Farmers who had observed the surveyors studying the positions of certain stars later gave the site its name.

A creative use of serpentine stone enhances the windows of St. Paul's Reformed Church on Route 100.

Two handsome examples of serpentine stone mansions in West Chester.

Serpentine—a pale green stone that was once part of the ancient sea floor—became a popular building material in West Chester in the mid-1800s, thanks to the operation of two nearby quarries, one north of the borough and the other owned by the Brinton family quarried after the Civil War.

The number of classical-revival style buildings here including the courthouse and "Horticultural Hall," earned West Chester the title, "the Athens of Pennsylvania." The architect Thomas U. Walter was said to have developed this type of sparse classicism in keeping with the area's heritage of Quaker simplicity.

With the possible exception of the Schuylkill canal system of 1825 or the nation's first turnpike—now the Lincoln Highway—built as early as 1792, few events transformed the county as much as the coming of the railroad in 1830. By the late 1800s, small rural stations like Pocopson enabled every farmer, shopkeeper and entrepreneur to market locally-made products to Philadelphia and elsewhere. The railroads also, of course, brought the world to Chester County.

Weathered stone walls and a pair of greyhounds grace the front entrance of The Big Bend, a 226-acre estate near Chadds Ford named for its location along the Brandywine. A turtle—a symbol of the Lenni Lenape Indian tribe—crouches near the door.

Indian legends and stories about former grave sites and Lenape villages abound in Chester County—this despite the fact that archaeologists haven't discovered any major finds since the late 1800s. Still, the owner of The Big Bend—George A. "Frolic" Weymouth, the founder and chairman of the Brandywine Conservancy—has a good reason for celebrating the estate's ties to a culture that virtually disappeared by 1735. The oldest part of the house once served as a trading post, and the surrounding land was said to be one of the tracts William Penn deeded back to the Indians in 1683.

◄ **Near the grand Georgian-style entrance of The Big Bend estate is a root cellar and a landmark statue of an Indian posed in a contemplative mood with a bow in one hand.**

The Indian monument in the White Clay Creek Preserve near the Maryland border is a tribute to the Native Americans who settled along the high knolls and ridges of a floodplain here. Settlements have been traced in the area dating back nearly 12,000 years.

The modest size of this church in Upper Oxford Township, founded by free blacks as the Hosanna African Union Methodist Church, hardly reveals its history as the hotbed of reform and a place that seemed to swell with activity as a former stop on the Underground Railroad.

Old Kennett Meeting and one of its celebrated stone walls which shielded a troop of American soldiers as they formed the first defense line during the Battle of the Brandywine in 1777.

Stone and brick Quaker meeting houses are found nearly everywhere in Chester County, but most are found in the southern townships where in the 1800s seventy-five percent of the population were said to be members of the Society of Friends. This heritage played an interesting role in the course of the county's history, particularly during the American Revolution. At the time of the Battle of the Brandywine, for instance, area Quakers were often divided over the issue of whether to hold to their pacifism beliefs. The members of Old Kennett Meeting chose not to show any sympathetic leanings even when they were interrupted in their midweek worship during the battle. With deliberate understatement, it was later noted in the meeting's records that "some disturbance" had occurred outside.

◀ **A giant oak evokes the spirit of the generations of Quakers who came to worship at the London Grove Meeting, first built in 1743 and expanded in 1818.**

Fence lines and a former boarding house form interesting outlines at Hopewell Village, a National Park Service site. Once one of several so-called "iron plantations," the site recreates Hopewell's zenith years when it sold iron stoves and other domestic items up and down the East Coast from 1820 to 1840.

A farm complex surrounds the "cast house," pictured here with the pointed stack of the charcoal-fueled furnace, where workers cast iron into stove plates and other goods.

Iron and steel have made Coatesville and Phoenixville famous, but for a long period from 1717 until the last iron ore mine closed in 1945, the "Iron Country" of Warwick Township was Chester County's most famous industrial region.

Throughout the 18th century, the region was ablaze with working furnances and forges and dozens of related industries—saw mills, iron ore mines and limestone quarries—which produced everything from iron nails and hinges to iron stoves and Revolutionary War cannon.

Although many of the early forge communities were later converted into large country estates, the region still reveals its history in its network of old transport roads and small dwellings that once housed miners, woodcutters and colliers who were responsible for the near round-the-clock clearing and burning of trees.

The former company store, shown here with a carriage house and the Reading Furnace Mansion which dates to about 1737, was once part of a bustling iron-making community. During the American Revolution, both Reading and Warwick Furnaces were government-designated arsenals. General George Washington spent two nights at the Reading mansion—along with about a thousand soldiers whose tents dotted the surrounding fields, and two hundred horses and cattle.

The south branch of French Creek cuts through the fields of Warwick Furnace Farm shown here in the distance. Below, the ruins of the Warwick Furnace. Its most successful product was a fireplace insert—better known as the "Franklin Stove"—invented by Benjamin Franklin who was a friend of the furnace owner.

The Hibernia Mansion stands on the edge of a 800-acre county park. It was given an elegant Georgian appearance in the 1920s.

The last visible remains of a forge built in 1790 vanished long ago at Hibernia. Only a few homes in the area date to the period in the 19th century when the Hibernia Iron Works was the center of a thriving community, surrounded by thousands of acres of woodlands. The ironmaster, Charles Brooke, built part of the present-day mansion. He later loaned money to Rebecca Lukens, a pioneer in her day for overseeing the operations of the nation's first boiler plate works. The mills, which straddle the west branch of the Brandywine in Coatesville, have been in operation since 1816. Rebecca took charge of the company after her husband, Charles Lukens, died in 1825.

The grand entrance of Graystone Mansion which was built in 1889 by Rebecca Lukens' grandson, Abram Francis Huston. As a partner in Lukens Iron & Steel Works, Huston was able to afford the best architects of his day, Cope and Stewardson. They were the designers of a style later dubbed collegiate Gothic, which they perfected at Bryn Mawr College and Princeton University.

"Instead of small features...it expands into the grandest sweeps, its hills are never too steep for the plough and rise in that bold round form which gives beauty to its picturesque appearance...." from the 1809 journal of Joshua Gilpin, describing an area of Chester County now dotted with Amish farms.

The Landscape

Chester County is a region of diverse character. The terrain varies from the steep hilly areas of the north and the boulder-studded range known as the Welsh Mountains, to a rolling countryside that gently tapers into the Delaware River basin in the south. It is a region of horse farms and company steel towns, 18th-century homes and tourist attractions. Few places in Pennsylvania, or even in New England, have as many covered bridges, old mills, former one-room schools, and Quaker meeting houses as Chester County. Yet, it's a place that remains surprisingly orderly in its diversity. In the northern part of the county, the old homes made of tan and reddish fieldstone gradually give way to structures made of grey fieldstone or local brick, the latter known in southern Chester County as "brick boxes."

Perhaps the overriding impression of unity here is due to the early settlers' predilection for building structures in harmony with the landscape—a barn against the slope of a hill, for instance, or a house in the hollow of a field. Indeed, the everyday views of Chester County, shown in the following photographs, reveal an easy interrelationship between the county's history, agriculture, industry and art. The unifying impression is that one could not exist without the others.

The beauty of the area has drawn artists and landscape painters to Chester County since the early 1800s when regional painting revolved around the themes of the Hudson River School in capturing the rustic and the sublime. Along the Brandywine, with its mills and patchwork of fields and farms, the region exemplified the view of man living harmoniously with nature. Another generation of artists arrived in the early 1900s to study with Howard Pyle, a Wilmington-based illustrator who conducted a renowned summer school in an old mill along the Brandywine. Pyle's students included Maxfield Parrish and Jessie Willox Smith, but it was N.C. Wyeth who settled permanently in Chadds Ford and became the founder of one of America's best-known art dynasties. In painting the area's working farms, N.C. Wyeth developed a style of realism that combined a love of the countryside with the need to document the rural culture. His son, Andrew Wyeth, went one step further in capturing the region as a kind of microcosm of rural beauty. Today, even the Wyeth pallet has become universally recognized. It tends to be the same verdant greens, burnt umbers and sienna tones of the local orchard or "Indian" grass that skirts the hillsides here—colors that apparently captured the attention of the first settlers seeking arable land. Indeed, the lasting importance of agriculture in Chester County must have been on the minds of even the early government officials, who chose the image of a plow when they created the first county seal in 1683.

The richness of the soil was evident in the abundance of natural springs and the underlying areas of limestone which enabled nearly every farm to have a piece of meadowland. The word "meadow" today evokes a mental picture of cows or sheep grazing in the midst of a bright patch of greenery, but in the early days of settlement it was used to describe a more prosaic and specific area of the farm set aside as the "mowing ground" containing crops of clover or timothy. The success of these crops, along with wheat, rye, corn and flax, eventually led farmers to experiment with commercial products such as oats, the fuel for teams of horses or oxen, and barley, used to make malt for Philadelphia breweries. Some Chester County farmers even attempted, in the early 1800s, to explore the mysteries of silk-worm culture by growing Chinese mulberry trees among the usual fruit trees in their orchards. Although the silk-industry was short-lived, it is one example of the ways in which farmers here, particularly the Quakers, known for their interest in nature and scientific pursuits, constantly strove to improve the already bountiful land of Chester County.

Progress here can be summed up in a few succinct descriptions. In the 1700s, the county was an important source of wheat and rye crops—the "breadbasket of the colonies." By the mid-1800s, it became the land of "modern" dairy farms and cooperative creameries as well as the "beef-fattening capital of the nation." These two industries—dairy and beef cattle—seemed to reflect and determine the character of the local landscape in different ways. In the hilly northern townships, it was the cheerful presence of red or green-roofed farm buildings and the jigsaw-puzzle markings of dairy cows in a field while many floodplain meadows in the southern part of the county took on the appearance of the open Western plains, thanks to the introduction of crops like Kentucky blue grass and the solitary railroad spurs through the area.

One line that ran through southern Chester County—the Wilmington and Northern Railroad, established in 1869—not only connected myriad farm communities and tiny one-room stations that served as milk stops, but helped to spark the growth of local nurseries and hothouse enterprises. By the turn of the century, the county could easily have been called the "mail-order capital of the country," since so many products were shipped by rail, including the nation's first mail-ordered roses and nursery plants.

Agriculture remains an important industry in Chester County. But a farmer of the past would undoubtedly feel lost if he toured such areas as southern Chester County, which everywhere reflects the era of specialization. There are roadside "pick-your-own" orchards, sod farms, and scores of low-lying mushroom houses that have earned the county the title, "Mushroom capital of the world." Horse stables out-number dairy farms, and cattle operations tend to be virtual genetic labs and scientifically-based feed lots— not the gentlemen's farms or country estates of the 1830s.

The Amish who settled here after the World War I were better able to maintain large tracts of land and dairy farms than their predecessors, usually Quaker farmers who had smaller families and had other interests. In many areas today around Oxford and along the Octoraro Creek, the Amish farms impose a striking order on the landscape. It seems odd at first to see their immaculately-kept barns and white-washed farm buildings standing in the midst of bright green yards that have a tidy postage-stamp appearance. But then one realizes its not the farm's neat appearance that gives it away as Amish-owned, but the lack of telephone poles and overhead power lines.

What is really unusual about the county's agricultural history, though, is that it evolved at a time when Chester County had its own mini-version of New England's paper, steel, and textile "Industrial Revolution." Along the Brandywine and the French and Pickering Creeks, for instance, there were the requisite "company towns" and villages comprised of narrow row houses and double family homes where neighbors shared front porches and back alleys. Still, despite all the "progress," the county has remained surprisingly rural. For the most part, its industrial history is visible only in the remains of an old dam breast, a furnace ruin or the ghost of a mill race coursing through a pasture. One region north of the confluence of the east and west branches of the Brandywine, in East Bradford Township, is part of a 1,800-acre area recently placed on the National Register of Historic Places as a historic district for its early agrarian history and water-powered industries. It adjoins other districts of verdant glens and hillside farms, one appropriately named "Paradise Valley." Along with its old stone houses and bank barns, the region still reveals history in the maze of farm lanes linking neighboring farms and old estates. Many of these lanes are still used today by contract farmers to move machinery and equipment from one farm to another, as was the custom a hundred years ago.

Chester County is also a place where nearly everything has a history, or an explanation. Drive through any region of the countryside here, and you'll probably find a centuries-old oak tree growing in the middle of an open field or a lone sycamore tree—also called buttonwood by the longtime residents— standing like a sentinel over a spring house. The road itself may be sunken with age, its embankments rising and dropping in height as you travel along it. But winding roads that seem to jog randomly through a landscape are merely following old property lines, and the lone oak tree might be a rare survivor from the early days of settlement when clearing the land was often a haphazard and random chore.

Chester County colonists were said to have followed the Indians' advice in using sycamore trees, which grow in wet areas, to determine the best place to dig a well or build a spring house. They also tended to use the Indians' method of so-called "axe and hoe" farming in which crops were planted between trees girdled with axe cuts and then burned. The colonists also allowed their pigs, cows, horses and other farm animals to roam free (a court-appointed "ranger" kept track of strays and unbranded animals), which probably didn't improve the survival rate of young trees and seedlings growing in open fields.

But Chester County is also a place of unexplained and miraculous wonders. Tucked away on the southwestern edge of East Nantmeal Township, for instance, is the "Great Marsh," a 700-acre tract of tall grasses that is transformed each spring into an expanse of greenery and flowering plants. Its importance as a wetland and nesting haven for thousands of wood ducks, hawks and redwing blackbirds has made it a mecca for naturalists, botanists and scientists since the late 1800s. More than two-hundred varieties of flowering and wetland plants are found here, along with several rare and reclusive species: the colorful marsh butterfly flits into the area in June, and the marsh wren, usually seen darting to and from a self-appointed post on a branch or old fence post left standing in the water. Occasionally, even the endangered, seldom-seen bog turtle hauls itself out of the water for a sun bath on the surrounding mud flats.

The landscape of Chester County—with its mix of open countryside and wood-crowned hills—once reminded William Penn's fellow Quakers of their native England. But the Welsh and Scots could also identify with the county's hilly regions, dense with hedgerows, old woodlots and steep creek embankments. Even today, Chester County remains a place where the character of the land is determined by the people who have lived here, in many cases for generations. For them, landmark designations tend to be simple and unofficial. It's not just the towns or farms that are given names, but the hollows and abandoned hidden spots in the countryside—places like Opperman's Corner or Miles Spring, which can be found somewhere in the neighborhood of the Ryan family farm, still called that by residents even though the Ryans have long since moved away.

Residents here also are particularly zealous when it comes to preserving the land for future generations. In the late 1980s, an astounding eighty-one percent of the population voted on the passage of a farmland and open-space preservation program even though it meant raising their taxes substantially. Conservation groups such as the Brandywine Conservancy and the French and Pickering Creeks Conservation Trust work with residents to protect critical watershed areas and to place thousands of acres under easement and other types of protective restrictions. They have helped to identify historic structures and towns and have made Chester County second only to Philadelphia County in the number of sites on the National Register of Historic Places found in Pennsylvania. The county's park lands, nature trails and wildlife preserves help to protect other aspects of the county—its ancient mines and quarries, deep woods, beautiful streams and serpentine barrens.

A winding country lane follows the contours of a pristine landscape near Unionville.

Landscape painter Peter Sculthorpe is part of an artistic generation after Andrew Wyeth whose career has revolved around painting the people, customs and beauty of the local area. Idyllic spots along the Doe Run, shown here, are among his subjects.

Small white caps form on the east branch of the Brandywine above Downingtown. Local residents have yet to decide whether to call this force of rushing water that once powered nearly one-hundred and fifty mills a creek or a river.

A long curving section of the French Creek seems to drift through Warwick County Park near Coventryville. Along with the Pickering, the French Creek helped to shape the character of northern Chester County by providing water-power to many of its first iron works and later steel industries. Coventry Forge, built near the present-day park in 1718, was only the second forge established in Pennsylvania.

Lichen-covered rocks along the Falls of French Creek create an interesting abstract work of art. ▶

The clusters of blue bells that grow under a series of graceful dogwood trees at the Brandywine River Museum are emblematic of the delicate ecological balance of the Brandywine region.

Contour farming creates colorful bands in the countryside.

An Amish farmer in Honey Brook Township tends to his fields.

The Amish, once close neighbors with large Quaker communities in southern Chester County, uphold a similar belief in peaceful government and social harmony. They are able to maintain their stable life by placing the family and community above the individual. As they describe it, they must "live together, worship together, and work together."

Modern life must be constantly kept at bay in areas around Honey Brook where the number of "English" residents—as the Amish call their non-Amish neighbors—are beginning to out-number the "Gentle folk." Still, the Amish are able to maintain their close family ties through such simple means as building their schools within walking distance of neighboring farmsteads.

An Amish one-room school stands alone in a landscape. When school is in session, a peaceful atmosphere prevails—both in and outside the classroom.

The Doe Run bridge, built in 1820, had to be replaced in 1881. Judging from stone-embedded side ramps, there were once plenty of travelers through this area.

Twin covered bridges span the shallow, rocky-bottomed waters of the Doe Run and Buck Run creeks which merge in a beautiful, wood-crowned dell known as the Laurels Reserve, a 771-acre private nature preserve. Once part of a sprawling 11,000-acre cattle operation, the Laurels is tucked away in a far corner of West Marlborough Township and is managed and protected in perpetuity by the Brandywine Conservancy. Still found here are the groves of rhododendron and mountain laurel that gave their name to the pre-Civil War Laurel Iron works, now in ruins.

Open only to foot (and hoof) traffic, the twin bridges in the Laurels evoke a sense of timelessness and wonder. In the 1800s, there were ninety-eight covered bridges built in the county. Of these, only seventeen are still standing today and only twelve are open to traffic.

Wild dogwood blooms along the Doe Run.

The gentle confluence of the Doe Run and Buck creeks is one of many remarkable features of the Laurels, along with, of course, its twin covered bridges.▶

Each spring, the "Great Marsh" in East Nantmeal Township—pictured here where it borders a private farm near the headwaters of the Marsh Creek—is transformed into a waterworld of pale greens and flowering plants and is a nesting haven for wood ducks, marsh wrens, redwing blackbirds and other wildlife. Described as a rare example of periglacial marsh formed during the Ice Age, the marsh is protected by not one but three conservation agencies.

Small cattle operations with less than a hundred head of cattle, like this one near Doe Run, have helped to make Chester County one of the economically top ten counties in the state, generating $44 million in annual beef production revenue.

The verdant green countryside of West Marlborough provides a striking background for grazing cattle. Yet, the region is more than picturesque. Beginning in the 1830s, several factors, including the area's network of creeks and the introduction of crops such as Kentucky blue grass, brought the county fame as the "beef-fattening capital of the nation."

In recent years, life here has revolved around the operations of the Buck and Doe Run Valley Farms and a distinctive dark-red steer called the Santa Gertrudis. From 1946 until 1984, when the farm was sold, they were a fixture of the region, grazing on the 11,000-acre farm that served as the fattening or "finishing" operation for the acclaimed King Ranch in Texas. Today, lumbering herds of Black Angus are often found in the region, typically on small cattle operations called "seed" operations or cow-and-calf farms.

A classic pastoral scene from West Marlborough Township's "cattle country."

An early morning fog casts a mystical spell over a woodland in West Whiteland.▶

For years, bands of colorful rose fields, shown here bordering Route 796, have been the landmark of Jennersville, an unhurried little village between Oxford and Kennett Square.

The interconnectedness of the county's history is perhaps best seen in the growth of its nationally-known horticultural enterprises. The Swedes may have been the first settlers to grow orchards here, but it was the Quaker farmers living in southern Chester County in the 1800s who perfected the art of growing under glass, as hothouse enterprises were then called.

Groupings of long and narrow, windowless buildings scattered around the countryside near Kennett Square are a puzzling sight for those who don't know the area's reputation as the "Mushroom Capital of the World."

Roses, carnations, sweet peas, snap-dragons and tomatoes were among the first hothouse products. Curiously, the mushroom enterprises of today were reportedly once a sideline business of these early nurseries. It was said to have begun in 1885 when a group of Italian workers—their families came to the Kennett Square area as stone masons— began to grow mushrooms for their own use, taking advantage of the extra space found under the nursery benches.

Wildflowers form a blanket of color in Marsh Creek State Park.

◀ **A field of goldenrod highlights the whiteness of a distant barn near Oxford.**

Horses graze in a fog-shrouded meadow near Kemblesville.

An equestrian out for a morning ride in southern Chester County.

Although riding stables have only in recent years replaced the predominance of dairy farms, horses have had a long history here. Indeed, one of the first items on the William Penn's agenda was to round up all the additional "good" and "shapely" wild horses and to ship them for sale to Barbados. The 19th-century historians J. Smith Futhey and Gilbert Cope note that goats were among the first domestic animals in the colonies, but the "horse was the first in our county to receive special care in breeding."

The stable and rolling back pasture of the Brushwood estate near Malvern.

Brushwood Stable has been called the virtual shrine of Chester County's steeplechase community. That's because the owners of the estate, the Morans, have been long-time organizers of the popular Radnor Hunt Races, an annual steeplechase event. Brushwood's tidy grounds and beautiful old fieldstone stable— complete with dormer windows and frame cupolas—exemplify the old Chester County estates of the past.

Barely discernable, a lone fox pauses on a hilltop near Newark Road. ▶

The informally dressed "field" of the Cheshire Fox Hounds wait for a fox to be drawn from a covert in the midst of scenic woodlands and cornfields during cubbing season.

For more than half a century, Nancy Hannum, a petite woman known for her fierce protection of the area's unspoiled countryside, has been the fieldmaster of Mr. Stewart's Cheshire Foxhounds. The private hunt was established in 1912 and now meets three times a week, covering a vast territory of neighboring farms and private properties encompassing nearly 35,000 acres.

The riders who follow the hunt, better known as the "field," generally spend the day in quiet pursuit of the fox. Hannum, who now rides to the hounds in her signature jeep—doing everything short of jumping the fences—often stresses the sport's non-aggressive appeal. "The game today is the enjoyment one gets from seeing a wily, clever animal outwit a disciplined hound," she says.

A pair of iron foxes stand at attention on the pillared gates of Brooklawn, a 1,600-acre estate in Unionville owned by Nancy Hannum, the area's grand dame of fox hunting.

Huge hardwood trees closely line the banks of the Westtown Lake, creating a colorful mirror image in early autumn.

The sienna and umber tones of an exemplar Chester County autumn day along Route 842.

A solitary Amish farmer amid an expanse of fields. ▶

Dairy cows graze in an open field of an old family farm near Kimberton.

A working farm in many parts of Chester County today is likely to contain horses or beef cattle rather than dairy cows or potato fields as was the case in the years after the World War II. Pictured here is a farm in Londonderry Township.

Another workday is completed on an Amish farm in lower Oxford Township.

A glinting mosaic of towering trees, autumn leaves and sunlight creates
a serene setting along a tiny creek near Barr Road in Willistown.

Old ruins in a field near Unionville tell of a time when small tenant farms checkered the countryside.▶

Horses on a farm near Chatham become playful on a crisp winter day.

The mile-long fence of an estate in "hunt country" disappears into the morning fog. ▶

The Octoraro Creek forms a natural barrier between Chester and Lancaster Counties. Here it is spanned by a covered bridge as it runs through a fringe of woods near Atglen where many Amish settled after World War I.

Established in 1963, Nottingham County Park is Chester County's oldest park. Tucked away in a far corner of the county, near the Maryland border, the 651-acre park preserves a region that was once of little use to farmers: nickle and chromium mines pocketed the countryside and a swath of rocky ground—the Serpentine Barrens—extended for six miles over the region. Today, the area is compared to the Pine Barrens of South Jersey for its ecological importance.

A sunset on a crisp winter evening in Franklin Township.

◁ The aftermath of an ice storm: a crystal tree near Chatham.

A rider soars over an event fence at the Radnor Three Day Event.

People, Places and Events

Chester County is known for its beauty and diversity, but an equally attractive aspect of the region's character is its annual events and traditions—its people and places, for they are often interchangeable. The history of pastimes, after all, mirrors the interests of the ordinary citizen. It tells the story of how people spent their leisure time, and conversely, the kinds of jobs and particular lifestyle they had. Time, or lack of it, determined the course of many activities in Chester County, as it did in the rest of America.

In the 1800s, the lives of the residents were centered around farming which, in the days before mechanized milking and planting, left little time for any serious recreation.

Newspaper items of the period suggest that many pastimes had a dual purpose: Greased hog races and wrestling matches broke the monotony of a long day at a livestock auction, and impromptu foot or "sack" races kept farm boys occupied while their fathers waited their turn at the local gristmill.

Notices of debating societies, evening lectures and musical recitals suggest that the county embraced the intellectual and scientific movements of the day. But there was also the "old Quaker influence," as one newspaperman in 1875 put it, which tended to discourage residents from wasting their time on frivolous activities or extravagant social gatherings. In fact, the same journalist described the county seat as a place where "habits and customs were simple and quiet"; it was a place that was still lit largely by candlelight and where people went to bed early, although there were plenty of "oyster bars" and "unhorsed vehicles."

With the exception perhaps of the Fourth of July, there were few occasions when people gathered en masse and spent the day "toasting and feasting," as the "Jubilee of American Liberty" was often described. Even then, the holiday was sometimes celebrated in late July since harvest chores typically kept residents too busy to enjoy the day earlier in the month.

Chester County today seems far removed from the days when winter was known as the "dull" season and notices of railroad shipments such as the delivery of coal or cattle were avidly followed in the local papers. As Mike Biggs' photographs reveal, Chester County is a place of historic sites, parks, gardens and museums, as well as an almost endless array of annual events and public exhibits. So much of the area's identity is tied to its rural and artistic history (the term, "Wyeth Country" is a familiar expression) it seems fitting that activities here often range from the sublime to the spectacular—canoeing down the Brandywine, for instance, or visiting Longwood Garden's soaring glass conservatories filled with flowers and plants in the middle of winter.

Small towns no longer have their own community band, but the tradition of musicians getting together for a hoedown continues at Hibernia Park and at Jennersville's Sunset Park. Indeed, for the most part, the kinds of diversions people enjoyed in the past are not that different from those of today. Chester County is still home to the oldest outdoor horse show in the nation—the Devon Horse Show—and one of the oldest hunt clubs, Radnor Hunt, founded in 1883. Annual events still tend to revolve around community life or the celebration of the seasons.

Newspaper notices of the early part of the 19th century create a portrait of Chester County as a hopping social place. In winter, there were bachelor balls, skating parties, square dancing, and corn-husking parties. Although such activities helped lessen the feelings of rural isolation, they were not always viewed as mere social events. The chopping matches that brought neighbors together each autumn, for instance, also accomplished the necessary task of building up the winter wood pile. Many after-harvest activities were regarded as appropriate forums for courtship. German-American residents often held apple butter-making parties and apple-peeling gatherings known as snitzing parties, which often lasted far into the night. Given the steamy process of boiling down apples, couples also had the perfect excuse to leave the party and step outside. There was even a courtship ritual associated with corn-husking: tradition has it that if a man discovered a red ear of corn, he earned kisses from all the ladies.

A survey of the various activities held in the small town of Byers, in northern Chester County, on the other hand, suggests that pastimes are not so easily categorized. A notice in 1908, for instance, announced that a "mock trial" would be held in the town of Byers to help solve a neighborhood dispute. A few years earlier, Byers residents were occupied with an entirely different activity: digging up their fields in search of newly-discovered veins of graphite, then called plumbago. Residents were also urged to hear "Paul, the Tramp Preacher" in a public sermon at Ives' lumber yard; and they considered forming a "Horse Company" or "Vigilant Association" dedicated to the protection of horses, as West Chester residents had done.

In 1819, Chester County residents could travel by train to Philadelphia and hop a steamboat to Cape May, but that year also drew crowds in West Chester to see the arrival of the newfangled velocipede. That event was followed a few months later by an elephant, on view for 25 cents. There was no charge, though, to see the aeronaut who manned the large hydrogen-filled balloon, The Rio Grande, in 1856; however, a notice stated that "an extra quarter or levy" would not be turned down.

A paper trail of many of the old-time events is found in the Sanderson Museum in Chadds Ford where entire walls are plastered with posters and handbills announcing the appearance of Chris Sanderson, the legendary fiddler. Sanderson, a former school teacher, seemed to appear at every grange-, fire hall-, and fairground-gathering in existence in the 1940s and '50s.

Living by the seasons instead of by the factory clock, residents of the past tended to approach even team sports on an informal basis. Baseball clubs were first formed in the 1850s, but they had no set schedules and games were generally conducted as challenges between teams representing neighboring towns. After the Civil War, baseball games became more competitive and standardized as the game evolved from a regional preoccupation to a national craze. Area companies also took up the idea of sponsoring teams to improve labor-management and community relations. The Parkesburg Iron Co. even built a state-of-the-art stadium, complete with dugouts, and invited the Phillies, the Boston Red Sox, the Detroit Tigers and other big league teams to play the company's team.

In addition to a love of sports and the outdoors, the sheer amount of documentation and artifacts now found in places like the Chester County Historical Society indicate that the county was settled by a community of "savers" and recorders. In recent years, the emphasis on history and community ties is apparent in the proliferation of various "Days" honoring a township's colonial past or founding. Indeed, despite the fact that residents here have never been able to agree on calling the Brandywine a creek or a river, few areas have such a strong sense of identity as Chester County, home to such traditions as Chester County Day, an annual tour of old homes and landmarks that has taken place—rain or shine—every October since 1940. Residents also keep current about their county's past through walking tours, open houses, and even re-enactments.

One of the largest "staged" events takes place at the Brandywine Battlefield Park in Chadds Ford, where hundreds of Red Coats and Continentals convene each year to recreate a battle that took place on a sweltering September day in 1777. Ellen Carmody, who chairs the reenactment group, Revolutionary Times, calls the battle a virtual "Who's Who" of the war. Others have called it the largest gathering of troops in the American Revolution. Its impact on the region was so lasting that one historian, Henry Seidel Canby, recalled that local residents routinely dated events in their lives from September 11, 1777.

Thanks to the foresight of a group of local residents who formed the Valley Forge Centennial Association in 1877, enough physical evidence of the historic encampment was saved that it eventually led to the creation of the Valley Forge National Park. The group, comprised mostly of women who modeled themselves after the Mount Vernon Ladies' Association, focused their initial efforts on purchasing General George Washington's headquarters, which was owned by a widow who demanded the then inconceivable sum of $6,000 for her modest home. In raising the funds and opening the headquarters to the public, the association ensured that the history of Valley Forge did not simply vanish. Less than a hundred years after the American Revolution, Valley Forge was better known as the site of a pioneering steel town which stood at the center of a busy canal and rail service. Visitors came to see the area's labyrinth of caverns discovered during quarry operations, or to attend lectures held at a utopian industrial village whose members promised to be "moral, sober, and industrious."

The Devon Horse Show reportedly began in 1895 as a challenge to local farmers to try their hand at horse breeding, since horses were then declining in number. As more Philadelphians moved to suburbs, converting former summer homes into grand estates, more horses were needed for recreational pursuits. The popularity of after-work carriage drives and weekend fox hunting, in particular, determined the broad focus of the show, which remains open to many horse breeds—saddle horses, hackneys, hunters, and Shetland ponies. The annual steeple-chase event at Radnor Hunt, on the other hand, was established by members of the hunt club who were looking for some excitement when the hunting season ended after Easter. They chose the English tradition of steeple chasing—named for the practice of racing horses from one distant church steeple to the next—and modified it for their own use here. The one-day event today consists of seven grueling races and routinely draws 20,000 spectators each year.

In the early 1800s, botanists and nurserymen from around the world came to a small Quaker farm thirty miles west of Philadelphia to see, amid fence lines and grazing livestock, a 15-acre oasis of unusual ornamental trees and tall pines smartly laid out in parallel allees.* This early arboretum, known as Pierce's Park, is now part of Longwood Gardens, which were open to the public in 1921 by Pierre S. du Pont. He had purchased the property in 1906 in "an attack of insanity," as he later called it. Today, Longwood remains true to the vision of its creator—to showcase what can only be described as the best and the brightest of the plant world.

Washington's Headquarters was one of the first restoration projects, purchased from a widow in 1878 for the then unheard of sum of $6,000. The campaign was led by a local group, the Valley Forge Centennial Association.

Although the Valley Forge National Historical Park commemorates the Continental Army's hardships during the winter of 1777-78, the estimated seven million annual visitors generally forgo authenticity to enjoy the park in spring or summer.

A winding boulevard and a series of paved walkways connect areas of the 3,000-acre park where soldiers once encamped amid a patchwork of local farms and an area practically barren of trees with sweeping hay fields and crops of wheat, barley and rye.

The 18th-century farm houses that served as Washington's headquarters and Varnum's quarters have been restored, along with a commissary and much of the military works used by the Continental army.

A replica of one of the original log huts, pictured here with a couple of sightseers. Nearly 2,000 huts were built under General Washington's orders after an unexpectedly harsh snowfall in December, 1777.

Valley Forge Park's restored buildings and granite memorials tell the story not only of the winter encampment but its history as the nation's first military training ground. Nearly 11,000 Continentals were trained, much like the British, in military tactics and formal rank or columnar movements which determined the outcome of the American Revolution.

A row of cannon overlooking an expanse of open land creates a spot for reflection.

Riders make their way toward a restored spring house at Valley Forge. In recent years, selected areas of the park have been allowed to revert to meadow. ▶

The tale-tell signs of a three-day event—red and white course flags, sturdy fences and an eagle-eyed fence judge—are all evident in this view of Radnor's international three-day competition.

The spacious, hilly terrain of the Radnor Hunt Club grounds is the site of a number of annual events long associated with the old landed dynasties of the Main Line horsey set. The club itself is one of the oldest and longest-standing fox hunting clubs in the country, having been founded in 1883. But there are also steeplechase and three-day events here, with jumping courses that extend over several miles.

Developed as an endurance sport to test horse and rider cooperation and fitness level, the three-day event includes dressage, a cross-country course and stadium jumping. Radnor's cross-country is a grueling event that is timed and designed to include obstacles made of natural materials such as a deep stream or a steep hill, replicating what a rider might encounter in "hunt country." Above, the timed jumping event. Below, a dressage competitor.

Steeplechase events like the Radnor Hunt Races and the Race for Open Space draw crowds who not only share the excitement of one of America's most competitive sports but a love of preservation. Both events benefit the Brandywine Conservancy, the environmental organization in Chadds Ford.

◄ Rider and horse speed through a water jump at the Radnor Three Day Event held in October, typically against a stunning backdrop of autumn colors.

Horse and rider clear an obstacle at Devon. This one appears to be a tribute to the windsurfers at the Marsh Creek Reservoir.

Long billed as the "Place Where Champions Meet," the Devon Horse Show is considered one of the country's greatest outdoor jumper showcases. The Budweiser Grand Prix class alone offers $50,000 in prize money. Olympic hopefuls frequently compete at Devon to become eligible for a place on the United States equestrian team.

◄While generations of riders have paraded past the judges' stand in the legendary "Dixon Oval," the main arena at Devon, certain events ebb and flow in popularity. Pictured here is the stadium-filler of recent years—show jumping.

Horse and rider clear a fence in the main competitors' ring, the Dixon Oval. Below, amid Devon trophies is a tray of lemon sticks, a traditional delight of the fairgrounds.

A class of young riders parades slowly around the Dixon Oval, above, in the always endearing class known as Lead Line, open to toddlers and youngsters under the age of six. Opposite, a young rider maintains her poise. Because they are too young to ride without assistance, Lead Line participants are judged on how well they sit in the saddle as well as the suitability of their pony. Below, some special awards are given, but in the end each rider receives a blue ribbon and—perhaps the most anticipated award—a lollipop served on a silver tray.

A century ago, Devon's coaching classes focused primarily on the horse so that breeders could compare notes in different divisions such as the light and heavy-harness types and the all-purpose "roadsters." Today, classes like the Coaching Obstacle Trials and the Coach Horn Competition highlight the skills needed in maneuvering and signaling.

A coaching "appointments" class at Devon offers a mini-history lesson in the selective colors and detailing of a well turned-out carriage. The gleaming and meticulously painted carriage door, below, recalls the days when artists coveted apprentice jobs with local coach and sign shops.

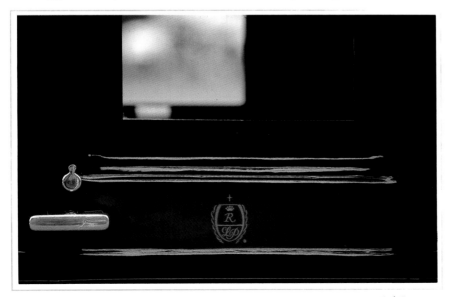

The artist Jamie Wyeth shares a passion for carriage driving, viewed by many neighbors along the Brandywine as the perfect means to appreciate the rhythms of the woodland trails or the area's gently rolling hills.

The day before the Winterthur Museum's annual point-to-point races—the last of a series of springtime hunt meets in the Unionville area—a celebrated ritual takes place on the property of Jamie Wyeth who is joined by friends and neighbors in the traditional crossing of the Brandywine. The event ceremoniously recalls a day in 1966 when Wyeth's neighbor, George A. "Frolic" Weymouth, invited area landowners on a carriage ride and picnic to raise funds to establish the Brandywine Conservancy. Under Weymouth's leadership as chairman, the Conservancy has preserved more than 25,000 acres of land in the Brandywine region.

In recreating the original carriage ride, guests must navigate a maze of mowed grass created by George A. Weymouth, below, known for his ebullient personality and illustrious parties.

Hooves pounding, mallets flying, riders and ponies create acts of mayhem over a small white ball at the Brandywine Polo Club.

Barn swallows are known to swoop and dart over the surrounding corn fields of the Brandywine Polo Club in the tiny southern Chester County community of Toughkenamon (which wasn't named for this tough sport). But otherwise, the atmosphere of this club every Sunday afternoon is as exciting and professional as any polo club in Palm Beach, Newport or Saratoga, to name a few of popular polo spots in the country. While spectators "tailgate" or picnic along the sidelines, the sounds of thundering hoofs, and players whacking and swinging at a ball fill the air.

A day at the races: Dressed in their customary electrifying colored silks, a row of jockeys prepare to sail over one of dozens of high fences at the annual Pennsylvania Hunt Cup Races.

Dogwoods bloom along a circular path. Such garden "rooms" are found throughout Longwood's 1,050 acres, many of them created with wisteria arbors, enchanting allees, ponds or fountain terraces. ▶

Towering structures in Longwood's Topiary Garden create an atmosphere right out of Alice in Wonderland.

Longwood Gardens enchants an estimated 800,000 visitors a year with its array of gardens and displays ranging from Versailles-style fountains and centuries-old woodlands to formal garden walks and lush re-creations of the tropics. Longwood's expanse of interconnected conservatories—famous for their high ceilings, domed-shaped forms like structures in a turn-of-the-century world's fair—were built by Pierre S. du Pont in 1921.

Behind the scenes, troops of workers continually test new arrangements and plant varieties grown in the hot houses or discovered on plant-gathering expeditions—Mediterranean plants are the latest craze—all in the spirit of Pierre du Pont, a consummate planner and innovator who once toured fifty French chateaux and gardens in a single two-week trip.

Longwood is renowned as a place to learn, reflect, relax and, of course, photograph its multitude of plants and flowers. Below, the main conservatory.

Early April brings new arrangements and groupings of perennials to the outdoors. Here tulips peek out from a ground cover of grape hyacinth.

The white forms of calla-lilies stand out among the dark greenery of springtime plantings.

Late April brings colorful bands of tulips along a stately area known as the Flower Garden Walk.

Only Longwood can take an ordinary marvel like the tulip and create a stunning display of color and fragrance.

Countless man-hours go into these starry displays, brightening Longwood during special annual celebrations such as the Festival of Lights, above, and the Festival of Fountains, below, which draw visitors from around the world.

Longwood's Christmas celebration each year revolves around a theme and typically features choral and organ concerts, spectacular hanging displays, topiary creatures and giant trees made entirely of plants and flowers.

Boy with Hawk, a work in bronze by sculptor Charles Parks, greets visitors at the entrance to the Brandywine River Museum.

Sculptor J. Clayton Bright's cow, placed near the graceful bend of the Brandywine River, perfectly captures the benign and placid nature of bovines.

Summer at the Brandywine River Museum is heralded by clouds of butterflies that pick their way among the wildflowers and native plants growing in the museum's sunny gardens. Appropriately, the outdoor sculpture placed here and there along different paths reflect the natural and historic character of the region. The work is also a reminder that landscape painters of the Brandywine School are not the only artists inspired to depict the region in realistic terms.

Visitors quietly peruse paintings in The Andrew Wyeth Gallery.

The Brandywine River Museum is the country's largest depository of the work of the Wyeth family, particularly N.C. Wyeth and Andrew Wyeth. It has also in recent years expanded its role as a research facility for Wyeth scholars and art historians. Yet there is much art to be seen here that also encompasses the unfolding tradition of landscape painting over the course of more than two centuries.

Verdant scenes of Chester County which show a hillside view of miniature farms with tiny roads or sweeping fields scored with cut wheat reveal the penchant among 19th-century painters—among them, William Trost Richards, Thomas Doughty, George Cope—to celebrate nature, agriculture and commerce, at times all in the same picture.

Displayed among three generations of Wyeth art, Portrait of a Pig by Jamie Wyeth, Andrew's son, has become a perennial favorite among visitors.

In the recently acquired N.C. Wyeth studio—a gift to the museum from the Wyeth family—a still-life arrangement illustrates the artist's lifelong concern for historic accuracy. Of all of Howard Pyle's students, Wyeth was perhaps the most acclaimed and an avid follower of Pyle's method of using props not as an artistic crutch but as a means of developing a vivid pictorial imagination. Pyle advised, "Live in your picture—become one with it—feel its mood and action in every part of you."

The colonial John Chads House, once the home of the owner and operator of the first ferry to cross the Brandywine, was restored in the early 1970s.

The John Chads House stands on a knoll above a spring house and the headquarters of the Chadds Ford Historical Society, well known for its "living history" programs. On weekends from May through September, interpreters in period dress recreate the life of the early ferryman's household by greeting visitors with stories about their day or farm chores. Some interpreters even bake loaves of bread in a cellar kitchen supplied with a rounded-back "beehive" oven.

The Dilworthtown Inn stands amid a cluster of historic buildings.

Located just beyond the hectic rumbling traffic of Route 202, Dilworthtown was one of the county's first historic communities to undergo a major restoration effort and be placed on the National Register of Historic Places. In the 1960s, many of the buildings had fallen into disrepair, and the village was in danger of being forgotten as a Revolutionary War landmark—the site of a major British store house and five-day encampment after the Battle of the Brandywine.

The Battle of the Brandywine lives on: Rounds of musket fire, battle cries and booming cannon capture the mood and atmosphere of a long-ago day in September, 1777. ▶

Time-out: a group of "Red Coats" share their knowledge of musketry with a group of children as part of the regular camp activities of the park reenactment.

Although the "real" Battle of the Brandywine took place over a ten-square-mile area, the hundreds of re-enactors who convene each year at the 50-acre Brandywine Battlefield Park in Chadds Ford are skilled in conveying the critical factors of a battle that was determined largely by the character of the land. In Washington's day, the rolling countryside, punctuated in places by low-lying roads and river gorges, provided plenty of military obstacles.

Life off the battlefield is also re-enacted with numerous "camp followers" including drummer boys, field hospital workers, and women, generally the wives of the soldiers in the regular army who were often on the road for months.

In a clearing on the grounds of the Brandywine Valley Association, dozens of children and adults link arms and follow leaders in an event honoring the Lenni-Lenape Indians.

The Brandywine Valley Association, or BVA, as most residents here call it, was established in 1945 to protect the Brandywine which was then the main source of drinking water for the Wilmington area. The nation's first watershed authority, BVA created Marsh Creek Lake among other reservoirs and flood-control projects.

Today, education is the main function of the BVA; programs on farming, nature, and conservation are held at its 212-acre farm south of West Chester. In celebrating the history and beauty of the Brandywine, seasonal events tend to revolve around honoring the Lenni-Lenape Indians who once lived in summer settlements scattered along its banks.

Canoeing on the west branch of the Brandywine south of Coatesville.

Canoeing the Brandywine has always been a popular pastime in Chester County, but in recent years it has become a virtual rite of passage for people who have lived in the area for any length of time. Many partake in the experience with the help of the Northbrook Canoe Co. which has private right-of-way agreements at seven spots along the west branch, perhaps the most scenic part of the Brandywine.

The Struble Trail, dedicated by the county in 1979, follows a wooded and sun-dappled course along the east branch of the Brandywine. Pictured here is a section near Downingtown where the ruins of an early forge are found.

The 535-acre lake at Marsh Creek Park looks as tranquil and timeless as any natural lake, but it was actually created in 1974 to serve as a reservoir for area municipalities. It may be the area's most popular man-made lake, surrounded by nature trails, picnic areas and piers for boating and fishing. Wind surfers find the lake an especially outstanding summer oasis.

A peaceful spot in the Great Valley Nature Center, located in Charlestown Township known for its groves of sycamore trees and small pastures along the Pickering Creek. The township may be the only place named after the given name of its founder, Charles Pickering, who was among the passengers on William Penn's maiden voyage. ▷

The bed & breakfast business in Chester County has flourished in recent years, thanks to the number of historic homes open to the public. This one is called Faunbrook, once the residence of Smedley Darlington, a celebrated congressman known as the "autocrat of Chester County." His daughter, Isabel Darlington, was the county's first female attorney.

Inside and out, Faunbrook is considered one of West Chester's finest examples of an Italian Federal-style home, built in 1860. Shown here is one of the parlors of the seven-bedroom mansion. Now used as a reading and gathering area for guests, it looks as though a member of the Darlington family only momentarily left the room.

Climbing trees at Springton Manor Farm, a 300-acre county park near Glenmoore listed on the National Register of Historic Places.

With its immaculately maintained farm buildings, fence-lined pastures and assortment of outbuildings, Springton Manor Farm, opposite, looks from a distance like a farm from another century. Its name dates to a period when it was one of several manor houses on an eight-thousand acre tract held for proprietary use by William Penn.

Three-hundred Penn Oaks are still found on the property which became a county park in 1988. An agricultural museum traces watershed years of the area from 1800 to the 1850s, while the surrounding working farm offers a little hands-on experience. Depending on the season, visitors are encouraged to take part in maple sugar collecting, hay rides, sheep shearing demonstrations or harvest activities.

Chickens are part of a menagerie of farm animals found at Springton Manor, other animal friends include Tom, a bronze-colored turkey; Agnes, a formidable white pig; Cruz, the quarter horse; and Hamburger Patty, a black Angus steer.

The Phoenixville mural, which is almost three and a half stories high and eighty-feet long, is located in the heart of the city's shopping district.

Like many community projects, the creation of the Phoenixville mural took months of planning and countless neighorhood meetings. Phoenixville's former steel workers, business owners and long-time residents gathered to share memories and to determine the content of the mural which documents the days when steel was king and neighborhoods hopped with energy. During the city's heyday, the mix of languages and nationalities included Italian, Irish, Polish, Slovak, Ukrainian, and Hungarian.

Flying 18th-century style: these gently floating neon-colored craft are a familiar site on fair-weather days in Chester County. Because landings are arbitrary, the pilots who work for area ballooning companies generally offer a bottle of champagne to the owner of the property where they land.

Surrounded by a group of visitors on a free walking tour sponsored by the county, a volunteer relates the history of Breesey Court, a turn-of-the-century home in Downingtown noted for its formal courtyards and gardens.

The Edith P. Moore schoolhouse, part of a historic complex in Lionville listed on the National Register, was restored by the community in 1975.

Walking tours, open houses and community museums are just some of the ways the historic and scenic character of Chester County is celebrated. Indeed, few places can boast such traditions as Chester County Day, an annual tour of old homes and landmarks that has taken place—rain or shine—each October since 1940.

Groups like Uwchlan Township's historic commission hold frequent open houses and tours. One of its buildings, the 1859 Edith P. Moore schoolhouse in Lionville, exposes visitors to the rigors and delights of a one-room school education—pumping water by hand, taking notes on a slate board or daydreaming in the window-lined school room.

**Parks like this one—a wooded area of Hibernia County Park—offer
Chester County residents a variety of recreational activities...or
simply, a quiet place for a walk.**

Chester County is strengthened

by its variety of businesses

and attractions...

partners in progress

The Chester County Economic Development Council

Established more than 46 years ago by a group of perspicacious business leaders, the Chester County Economic Development Council has prospered over time – as has its host county.

At last count, the Council has succeeded well during its existence, creating over 75,000 new jobs, retaining over 110,000 existing jobs, helping to establish more than 5,100 new businesses and securing over $4.5 billion in low-cost loan financing for clients.

Clearly, those achievements weren't accomplished over night. And, certainly, a

Chester County really didn't grow beyond a cluster of small villages along its waterways until the 1800s. Some say it was the Quaker spirit and tradition of restraint, contemplation and caring that fostered those early patterns of habitation where the boroughs were situated along former Lenni Lenapi Indian trails and all the land in between was devoted to agricultural production. The family farm ruled supreme and the boroughs of Chester County existed to serve the needs of family farmers. Indeed, the farmers "went to town" to secure supplies, do banking and assorted tasks, and bring their produce and harvests for processing and shipping. Mills were situated along the rivers and streams; and,

Wanting to avoid the development errors of our contiguous counties, those sagacious business leaders previously cited formulated their vision for Chester County that sounded something like this: preserve the open spaces and vistas, they can never be replaced. Diversify the industrial basis – steel making won't last forever. Create outstanding educational institutions including colleges and school districts. Retain the history and tradition of the early settlers. Sustain agriculture as a principal endeavor. And, most importantly, establish a commitment to economic development that is "smart," environmentally sound, and self perpetuating. The Chester County Economic Development Council was their answer, their brain child and their tool for assuring that their vision would perdure for generations.

The Council, then, was vested with the responsibility of ensuring a healthy and prosperous economic climate for the residents of Chester. Today, the Council addresses its mission by offering start up businesses and Fortune 500 companies alike outstanding corporate sites, appropriate facilities, low-cost financing, agricultural development services, capable and highly-trained employees, and ready access to regional, national and world trade markets. The Council also obtains and administers grants for commercial and agricultural development. It seems that the only "development thing" the Council doesn't do is residential development – it's not part of its mission.

Chester County Economic Development Council headquarters, Exton, PA. Photographed by Angela G. Kelley

From a bottom line perspective, the net impetus of the Council's services focused on job creation, the generation of tax ratables, and the betterment of the quality of life for county residents. When you ride around the county with Gary Smith, the Council's President and CEO, you quickly get the feeling that there isn't a company, institution, or community that hasn't benefited in some way from Council services. Pointing out his car window, Gary will say: "we helped them acquire that corporate head-quarters site," or "they got their capital funds from us," or "that school used the Council for a bond issue." It's amazing how many companies and organizations have been touched by the Council and then went on to become enormously successful icons of their communities and major employers in the County. Some have

lot of sweat, knowledge, and compassion was invested in the process by Council staff along the way. To best understand the Council's roots and rites of passage, we need to start at the beginning, when Chester County was primarily agrarian, often regarded as a sleepy, exurban, Quaker community that most people wouldn't even know about if they didn't travel the Lancaster Pike or the Pennsylvania Railroad to get points west. Founded in 1682 by William Penn as one of Pennsylvania's original three counties,

when the railroads came, they established depots in the boroughs.

Fast forwarding from those early times, the period of 1900-1950 was pivotal to the economic development of Chester County and the emergence of the Council. Steel making was king, agriculture was the largest employer, and Philadelphia had already spilled over into Bucks, Delaware and Montgomery County causing the spread of the dreaded urban sprawl.

become household names, like Vanguard, Cephalon, CTDI, Herr Foods, West Chester University, Chester County Hospital, and Downingtown Borough.

In many ways, the Council truly is a unique organization. Founded as a private, non-profit corporation recognized by the Commonwealth of Pennsylvania, the Council is approved as a 501(c)(6) by the IRS. Perhaps it should be described as a private non-profit that provides a public service. There is no question that Chester County government and the leaders of the 73 municipalities in the county rely heavily on the Council and regard it as the "go-to" agency where economic development is concerned.

So how does the Council really operate? For one thing, the Council acts as an information clearinghouse providing both private and public sectors with requisite data. The Council also is a facilitator, constantly implementing economic development projects at the request of vested-interest parties. At other times, the Council functions as an interlocutor or "hand holder," bringing organizations together and assembling needed resources to foster economic development. And then the Council is a proponent, urging those with resources, capital, ideas and clients to pursue their commonalities collectively. Always, the Council is there, with 17 highly-motivated, extremely-experienced, listening staffers ready to go-to-bat for a worthwhile project.

In its infancy, the Council was called upon to assist companies in relocating to designated development areas strategically located throughout the county. Accordingly, the Council focused on marketing those sites by working directly and diligently with corporate executives, municipal authorities, and developers. At the front end of this process was the notion that business growth could be encouraged without becoming deleterious to maintaining the historic and environmental attributes of the communities in which the corporate sites are located. Then the phenomenon of compulsive comparison took over and today, over 45 corporate parks are located across the county which are specifically situated so as not to impinge on the quality of life.

Eagleview Corporate Park, Exton, PA

CCEDC works hard to advance the business of agriculture.

With the growth of corporate entities in the county, the Council was asked to deal with workforce questions such as: "if I move to the county, how will I attract, train, and retain employees?" The Council's approach, to create partnerships of training providers, marshall the forces of the state employment agency and CareerLink, and secure external grant funding for workforce development, quickly emerged. Over the years, the Council established the Chester County Workforce Partners, comprised of various training and employee support organizations, to assist companies with workforce development programs. Soon, state and federal grants were received, making over $11 million available for employee skills capacity building and incumbent worker training. Now, when a prospective in-migrating company seeks help with workforce development, the Council has the answers.

In its first year, the Council relied largely on donations volunteered by its Board Members to operate. The budget was about $75,000. By 2006, the budget has grown to more than $1.75 million with support from the state, the federal government and the county. The Council gradually became a fee-for-service organization providing services based on a not-for-profit fee structure which allowed the Council to pay employees from the proceeds. That business model, which maximizes the resources of clients, sets the Council apart from other economic development organizations. Successful businesses understand the model knowing that their consultant dollars will go a long way when they invest in the Council.

It was also at this time that the Council established the first low-interest loan program offered by the state to manufacturing companies. To promote, market, and close these loans, the Council established the Chester County Industrial Development Authority (IDA) in 1967 and later the Central and Western Industrial Development Authority in collaboration with the county and local municipalities. The IDA loans plus federal industrial revenue bonds brokered by the Council have had a tremendous impact on company financing in Chester County. Over 125 such deals have been made, valued at a total exceeding $3.8 billion.

Soon other loan programs were being offered, most with interest rates below market-rate financing. Today, the Council and its affiliates broker over 30 different loan programs. One in particular, the Small Business Administration (SBA) 504 program, has become extremely popular with start-up and expanding companies that need to purchase property and equipment. The Council has done over 200 SBA 504 loans over the years that provided ready, low-interest capital for business development.

Under the leadership of the Council's current Vice President and COO, Michael Grigalonis, the Council has been recognized by various state and national organizations as a major trendsetter in economic development. The Council has been

instrumental in developing the Route 202 corridor as one of the nation's major concentrations of IT, biopharma, bio-med, and life science companies. At last count, over 375 large and small corporations now call Chester County home while employing over 55,000 well-paid workers. The Route 202 corridor also is home to four (4) universities who participate aggressively in transferring seminal technology to the corporate community. To expedite that transfer to the recipient companies, the Council maintains three (3) support programs: Industry Partnerships in Life Sciences and Information Technology, respectively; and a Keystone Innovation Zone (KIZ) for various industry clusters.

The Council also has been successful in addressing the unique requirements of the 16 urban communities located in Chester County, including the City of Coatesville. While each has individual needs, they all are characterized by depressed downtowns, unhealthy brownfields sites, flagging tax revenues, inadequate infrastructure, empty storefronts, serious unemployment, and diminished expectations. In response, the Council developed several programs including an entrepreneurial training and mentoring project during which incipient business owners acquire skills for running successful businesses before opening their companies along the mainstreets of the municipalities. During 2000-2006 alone, over 175 incipient entrepreneurs have participated in the project with over 45% opening businesses thus far. The Council also has opened satellite economic development services centers in four (4) of the most distressed communities: the City of Coatesville, and the Boroughs of Phoenixville, Kennett Square, and Oxford. These centers put Council services where they are needed most. Other urban-oriented Council activities involve the development of a commercial "gateway" center on the old Amtrak rail yard in the west-end of Downingtown Borough and the redevelopment/reuse of the old Lukens Steel plant in the City of Coatesville and South Coatesville Borough.

It seems like every year the Council rolls out a new initiative! During 2005, the Council was asked by the county to redevelop a brownfields site in East Fallowfield/South Coatesville Borough into a county Public Safety Training Facility (PSTF) in response to concerns relating to terrorism, and the need to properly

Genesis HealthCare building in Kennett Square, PA. Also home to one of CCEDC's satellite economic development centers.

train the county's 5,000-plus first responders (fire, police and EMT professionals). This $36 million project at build out in 2009 will train thousands of responders annually in state-of-the art classrooms and training modules including a burn building, transportation tunnel, and tank car scenario. Thus far, the Council has raised over $20 million in PSTF project funding, developed plans for the facility, purchased land, and broken ground for construction.

The Council also has pioneered the acquision of "conduit" grants for redevelopment wherein private and public developers of former industrial and brownfields sites can access state and federal grants for infrastructure, construction and fit out based on new job creation and prospective economic impact on blighted areas. In the

last three (3) years, the Council has received over $38 million in grants for 17 different clients who are committed to creating in excess of 780 new jobs in economically depressed communities.

The Council has not worked alone. Its economic development partners, some who are housed in the Council's new 12,000 SF headquarters in Exton, include the Ben Franklin Technology Partners, Kutztown University, Delaware County Community College, Delaware Valley Industrial Resource Center, PA CareerLink, and World Tract Center of Greater Philadelphia. Meanwhile, the Council has created several "affiliate" organizations to complement, enhance and expand its economic development menu of services. They include SEEDCo (South Eastern Economic Development Company) to offer SBA 504 loans throughout Pennsylvania; PA Grows to broker the state-funded First Industry Loan Program and related projects; and CCEDF (Chester County Economic Development Foundation), an IRSapproved 501(c)(3) to accept foundation grants for special projects.

What does the future hold for the Chester County Economic Development Council? Without question, the Council will continue its roles as guardian of the quality of life in Chester County, the source for business development, the go-to organization for economic development services, and the state's first agricultural economic development protagonist. The council expects to continue working with the county's boroughs to reduce unemployment and increase returns on taxes. It also will pay greater attention to transportation issues, international trade, its sister city/county programs, business retention, environmental protection, energy "harvesting," vocational education, and partnerships/alliances for economic development. Since the Council isn't into crystal balls, no one knows what initiative will be next. What the Council's staff does know, however, is that their professional lives certainly won't be boring; and, they like it that way!

Cephalon is a leading bio-pharmaceutical company founded in 1987 in Chester County by Dr. Frank Baldino, Jr. The company has grown to become a premier bio-pharmaceutical company with industry-leading growth and a presence in major markets around the world. Today, Cephalon is preparing a new portfolio of therapies with the promise to have a profound impact on human health and well-being.

Chester County recognizes the enormous promise that Cephalon and other life sciences companies hold for this region, for their potential to improve people's lives and to spur growth. That is why bio-pharmaceutical companies locate and stay here.

R&D companies like Cephalon benefit from an the abundance of university research centers in this region and draw from a talent pool of skilled workers. Governments have made long-term policy and investment commitments to the sector, supporting life sciences companies from start-up through product commercialization. Employees rate our region high for "quality of life" and "affordability."

Cephalon shares its success with its neighbors as a partner in business and community life. As Cephalon grew, the company expanded its world headquarters in Frazer and chose West Chester as the center of its global research and development activities.

There is no better place in the world for a life sciences company to locate than in Chester County.

Frank Baldino Jr., Ph.D
Chairman and
Chief Executive Officer

Brandywine River Museum

In 1971, a unique place for American art known as the Brandywine River Museum opened it doors in Chadds Ford. Incredibly, nearly 200,000 visitors "discovered" the museum that first year. Today, millions of visitors later, the museum is internationally known for its unique focus on the art of the Brandywine region.

Artists have been drawn to the area since the late 1800s, including painters from the Hudson River School. In the early 1900s, another generation of artists came here to study with the celebrated illustrator Howard Pyle. Rather than trying to replicate the encyclopedic range of many museums, the Brandywine River Museum concentrates its collection primarily on art related to this heritage and American art of the nineteenth and twentieth centuries.

Renowned works by The Wyeth family – N.C., Andrew, and James Wyeth, among them – and other artists from the Brandywine region hang near American still-life paintings, important landscapes, and the work of many of the country's best-known illustrators. The nearby N.C. Wyeth studio complements the museum's exhibits and innovative educational programs.

Visitors come here for the setting, though, as much as for the art. Housed in a nineteenth-century grist mill, the museum stands unobtrusively along the banks of the Brandywine where a nature trail weaves through a series of woodlands and open meadows.

There are also informal gardens full of wildflowers, native plants, and tall stands of indigenous trees – all carefully maintained by the museum's volunteers to serve as an educational resource for horticulturalists and naturalists and to inspire homeowners who may want to attract butterflies and hummingbirds into their gardens.

Inside the museum, three galleries have retained their original dark wooden beams, which contrast with the white plaster walls and natural pine floors. In the center of the museum is a striking circular staircase as large as a silo – and symbolic of the region's agrarian character and the mill's original purpose – that opens onto three gallery foyers. Here a dramatic expanse of glass walls offers a view of the peaceful waters of the Brandywine and the breathtaking landscape that inspired nearly two centuries of art.

It is the interplay of setting with the art of the Brandywine Valley – artists painting the local landscape and then their paintings in turn provoking an appreciation of the region – that drives the museum's pioneer approach in bringing art to the public.

Indeed, the museum's curators have managed to build a collection that gives the visitor a broad understanding of the remarkable art of the region that goes beyond regionalism. Although the subject is specific, art movements as diverse as American Impressionism and the social realism of the 1930s are represented.

The museum has earned its reputation as an important cultural institution – Smithsonian magazine once called it one of the country's "most popular rural art centers" – in part for its unparalleled collection of American illustration and its gallery devoted to the works of Andrew Wyeth. Few contemporary artists are said to have created works as instantly recognizable by the American public – and elsewhere, including in Russia and Japan – as Andrew Wyeth.

The museum regularly augments its permanent displays with a round of special exhibits and shows, some of them organized through major museums. Others highlight domestic art forms of the Brandywine Valley or media other than painting; exhibits of nineteenth-century tinware, early pottery, and Amish quilts, for instance, have been some of the "hit" shows of the past.

The Brandywine River Museum is part of the Brandywine Conservancy, a non-profit environmental organization that was founded in 1967 to help protect the very landscape that had inspired so many artists. At the time of its founding, the region's beauty and history was on the verge of being lost forever to rampant development and industrial "progress."

Working specifically in the Brandywine watershed, the Conservancy focuses its preservation efforts on a different kind of legacy: its open space, pristine waterways, and historic resources.

The staff at the Conservancy's Environmental Management Center, located within walking distance of the museum, performs a range of jobs such as assisting townships with open-space planning, landowners with conservation easements, and communities with placing sites on the National Register of Historic Places. In land preservation techniques, the Conservancy has served as a model in developing a variety of methods and programs. Tens of thousands of acres of critical watershed land alone have been protected, in perpetuity, by conservation easements donated to the Conservancy.

With their joint mission to "preserve, protect, interpret," the Brandywine River Museum and Conservancy hope to retain the unusual beauty of the region for the present and future generations.

Immaculata University

Immaculata University, a Catholic coeducational liberal arts institution, was founded originally as Villa Maria College. The institution was granted a college charter in 1920, making it the first Catholic college for women in the Philadelphia area. In 1929, the name was formally changed to Immaculata College to accommodate government regulations for the naming of the post office.

Immaculata's origins date from 1906, when the Sisters, Servants of the Immaculate Heart of Mary, purchased the present site in Chester County. Ground was broken for Villa Maria Hall (the central campus building) in 1908, and two years later, the massive stone walls were complete. The growth of Immaculata University over the past eight decades has been gradual, yet consistent. The initial 198 campus acres have grown to approximately 372, while the two original dormitory-classroom structures are now part of a fourteen-principal-building complex, representing a multi-million dollar investment.

The faculty consists of approximately 100 full-time priests, sisters, and laypersons; these educators uphold and enliven a tradition of educational excellence sustained within an environment of concern for and interest in each individual. The genuine personal concern shown each student in an atmosphere of respect, vitality, and warmth is one of the distinct characteristics of Immaculata. The University has been recognized as an outstanding institution representing the highest quality in offering individualized preparation for careers and service.

Resident and non-resident students receive, within the framework of a Judaeo-Christian academic institution, education and preparation for positions of leadership and responsibility in their adult and professional lives. In September 1969, the college introduced an evening division program of Continuing Education for both men and women in order to serve local community needs. In September 1977, the college initiated a master's degree program in Bicultural/Bilingual Studies in cooperation with Marywood College. In July 1983, three graduate programs were inaugurated, seeking to address the need for graduate education among adult students interested in part-time or full-time study in psychology, nutrition education, and educational leadership and administration.

In 1991, the Bilingual/Bicultural Master's Program became integrated into

Immaculata's Graduate Division, together with the addition of Music Therapy on the master's level and doctoral programs in Clinical Psychology and Educational Leadership & Administration. The college received final approval in 1994 from the Pennsylvania Department of Education for the doctoral degree program, Doctor of Psychology (PsyD in Clinical Psychology), and in 1997 for the EdD in Educational Leadership. In February 1999, the college received approval for a Master of Arts degree in Organization Leadership. In 2006, the Master of Arts degree in Organization Leadership was the first graduate degree program to be made available in an accelerated format. Approval was granted in 2004 for a Master of Science in Nursing (M.S.N.) degree. The latest doctoral program, added in 2001, is a PsyD in School Psychology.

In 1995, an accelerated undergraduate degree program (ACCEL®) was established in Organization Dynamics, a model for an innovative mode of delivery of major programs for working adults. In 1997, following the success of this first accelerated program, four more accelerated programs were introduced: Dynamics of Human Performance Management, Information Technology for Business, the Associate of Science in Business Administration, and the BSN in Nursing. The latter was accredited by the National League for Nursing in 1984 and has been offered in a traditional format for more than 16 years. In 2006, the B.A. in Organization Dynamics became the very first degree program completely offered online. To accommodate students from the entire Delaware Valley, the College of

LifeLong Learning has expanded to over 30 off-site locations.

As a result of its unprecedented growth, Immaculata needed to reshape itself. In July 2000, Immaculata adopted a three-college organizational structure, comprised of the Women's College, the College of LifeLong Learning, and the College of Graduate Studies. The Trustees of Immaculata, along with the administration, faculty, staff, and students believe that Immaculata was indeed ready to call itself a university. On August 1, 2002, Immaculata College officially became Immaculata University.

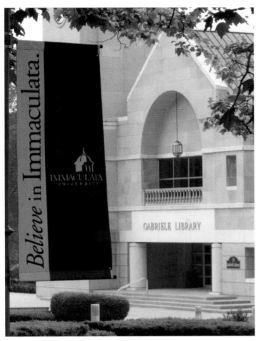

In October 2003, the Board of Trustees accepted several recommendations including inviting men to be a part of the College of Undergraduate Studies. In Fall 2005, Immaculata welcomed its first traditional-age, coeducational class into the College of Undergraduate Studies.

The powerful vision for national pre-eminence and the educational and structural changes that have ensued became more than mere words or convenience. To the team of high quality educators who make up the Immaculata community, these changes reflected the need to maintain individual attention to students in a dynamic and exploding world of information and change. The University believes that Immaculata students deserve no less than the best education that creativity, innovation, and sophisticated resources can provide.

The College of Undergraduate Studies

This college, comprised of approximately 750/800 full-time students, serves both men and women of all faiths and backgrounds. In a Catholic university, dreams are fired by spirituality, compassion, and creativity. More than 60 majors, minors, certificate, and pre-professional programs are available. To keep up with educational trends and student demand, new courses and degree programs are introduced regularly. The faculty and staff recognize the need to support and encourage the students to engage fully in life and learning. The spirit of challenge in this very energized environment creates an educational climate to produce the leaders of the future.

The College of LifeLong Learning

In the spirit of responsiveness to the special needs of adult learners, the College of LifeLong Learning provides an undergraduate, liberal arts education in traditional delivery and accelerated programs (ACCEL®). In addition, the college offers an extended array of non-credit seminars and workshops for personal and professional development to people in the workplace and in the community. Collaborative programs offered both on- and off-campus with corporations, school districts, and medical facilities, provide an opportunity for people in these areas to upgrade their skills or to attain higher degrees. Lifelong learners find in Immaculata a commitment to high quality education and need-sensitive preparation that allows men and women to achieve their potential for a meaningful future.

The College of Graduate Studies

The College of Graduate Studies completes the triad of the university model at Immaculata. The array of doctoral and master's programs, together with numerous post-baccalaureate workshops and enrichment courses, places this unit at the pinnacle of higher education activity. Immaculata offers doctoral programs in Clinical and School Psychology, and Education. Seven master's programs are also available including Educational Leadership & Administration, Music Therapy, Organization Leadership, Counseling Psychology, Nutrition Education, Cultural and Linguistic Diversity, and a Master of Science in Nursing. The College of Graduate Studies produces leaders – men and women who teach, who heal, and who serve in fields where the human element is paramount. The liberal arts core, required of all degree candidates, with its underpinning of ethical philosophy and servant commitment, prepares the Immaculata master or doctor to become a catalyst for good in a rapidly changing and sometimes violent world. With excellence as a standard and faith as a foundation, Immaculata graduates are offered the practical advantage of a quality education and the priceless heritage of values that prepare them intellectually and morally for the challenges of personal and professional life.

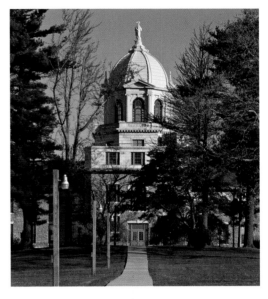

The University continues to expand and enrich program areas that have been successfully evaluated by the Middle States Association, the Pennsylvania Department of Education, and by learned, professional organizations related to specific areas. New degrees and programs are continuously being evaluated and instituted. Growth has been consistent over the University's eight-decade history with the student population growing to over 4,000 students. To accommodate the expansion of new students, Immaculata has designed a campus master plan and will be constructing new facilities over the next several years. For more information, visit www.immaculata.edu.

RE/MAX Professional Realty, Inc.

Kathleen McQuilkin, Janet Townsend & Tom McQuilkin
Outstanding Agents. Outstanding Results.

Buying a new home (or selling the current one) is among the most important financial decisions a family will make. Buying a new home here in Chester County will undoubtedly be one of the most rewarding decisions a family will make. And no one knows that better than Kathleen McQuilkin, Janet Townsend and Tom McQuilkin – the hometown real-estate professionals of RE/MAX Professional Realty, Inc.

As certified Realtors®, bound by a strict code of ethics that demands complete candor and always puts the needs of the client first, Kathleen McQuilkin, Janet Townsend and Tom McQuilkin share not only a wealth of experience and a proven record of expertise but also an unstinting affection for Chester County.

Self-described as "Chester County's biggest cheerleader," Kathleen McQuilkin, in fact, is Chester County born and bred, raised on a farm, where she began her lifelong love of equestrian pursuits. Licensed since 1976, she carries several advanced designations, including Graduate of the Realtors® Institute (GRI), Certified New Home Sales Professional (CSP), Certified Residential Specialist (CRS) and Certified Relocation Professional (CRP). A past president of the Chester County Association of Realtors® (2002), she is actively involved with the burgeoning Suburban West Realtors® Association, the Realtors® Legislative Alliance/Suburban Realtors® Alliance, and the Pennsylvania Association of Realtors®.

Kathleen's husband, Tom McQuilkin, is a native of Philadelphia, who moved to the county while in high school. Licensed since 1976, as well, he also holds a Bachelors degree in economics from St. Joseph's University in his home town. In addition to being a GRI and CSP, he holds a Pennsylvania state Appraiser license and a Broker license, the highest advanced designation a real-estate professional can hold. He also has extensive firsthand experience in building-and-ground development projects. As a Philadelphia native, who still delights in getting into the city for recreational and business events, or just to take in a ballgame, Tom admits that he finds it even more enjoyable to get back home to the beauty and serenity of Chester County – a emotion so many of his clients who have relocated here share.

Janet Townsend herself relocated here in the 1970s, and immediately decided never to leave the rolling green countryside of Chester County. A native of New Hartford, in upstate New York, where she taught elementary school, Janet worked in corporate America for more than a decade before returning to the real-estate industry. In addition to the advanced designations of CRP, CRS and GRI, she is also an Accredited Buyers Representative (ABR) and a Senior Real Estate Professional (SRES).

Their team member, Daniel Robins, holds the ABR designation and specializes in Buyer representation. He places special emphasis on caring for the concerns of first-time buyers and investors.

Certainly, one of Chester County's prime selling points is its desirable location. Situated just 30 miles from Philadelphia in the heart of the vast Boston-to-Richmond megalopolis, Chester County is less than three hours from Washington, D.C., to the south and New York City to the north. Also within easy reach: Lancaster

County's Amish country; the ski slopes of the Pocono Mountains; fishing, boating and beachcombing on the Delaware and Chesapeake Bays, and the Atlantic Ocean beaches of the Jersey shore. And needless to say, Chester County itself boasts unparalleled quality-of-life amenities, including restaurants to delight even the most discriminating palate, outstanding antiques shops and "shop 'til you drop" malls.

The county's robust business climate is another prime selling point, and in that regard, corporate employers can have every confidence that Kathleen, Janet, Tom and Dan will do everything necessary to guarantee that their most valuable assets – their employees – are comfortably settled here in Chester County, a beautiful place to thrive in. But whether it's a corporate employee relocating or a local homeowner trading up to her new dream house, clients can rest assured that these dedicated professionals will handle their real estate needs with the utmost care and attention.

All Realtors® are independent contractors, who put the needs and concerns of their clients above all else. Janet, Kathleen and Tom have chosen to affiliate themselves with RE/MAX Professional Realty, Inc., because RE/MAX helps them serve their clients even more efficiently. One of the most highly respected firms in the industry – and a strong supporter of local charities such as the Children's Miracle Network – RE/MAX offers its associates a wide array of support programs and educational opportunities to help ensure their professional success. The industry leader, not just in Chester County but worldwide, RE/MAX is a company founded on the practice of caring for its clients by setting its agents up to excel. The end result is that no one sells more real estate than RE/MAX.

The Chester County office of RE/MAX Professional Realty, Inc., is located at 557 West Uwchlan Avenue in Exton, Pennsylvania 19341. Prospective clients are invited to phone 610-363-8444 or 1-800-HOUSE-PA, and ask for Kathleen, Janet, Tom or Dan. Dan Robins, and Tom and Kathleen McQuilkin may be reached directly at 610-363-8672; Janet Townsend's direct line is 610-363-8436.

Tom McQuilkin

Kathleen McQuilkin

Janet Townsend

Willow Financial Bank

Willow Financial Bank
Community Bank, Community Dedication

At Willow Financial Bank, we believe that our customers - consumers and businesses – expect the product and service offerings of a larger bank, and also the customer service, attention to detail and familiarity with the community that can come with a smaller one.

Deeply rooted in the region, Willow Financial Bank has served the banking and financial needs of customers in Chester County for over 80 years. Today Willow Financial Bank, which at one time operated as the former Downingtown Building & Loan, provides the capabilities and advantages of a larger banking organization – loan, mortgage and deposit product options, expanded hours, local branches and access to investment professionals, and much more. The difference is, we know the communities we serve.

Roots in the Community

From the faces you see in local branches, to the management of the bank, Willow Financial knows what the residents of an ever-growing Chester County need. We live and work right along side our customers, and call many of them our neighbors.

This commitment to the local community has been a part of the bank for many years. The Bank's former CEO, and a visionary of today's Willow Financial Bank, Ellen Ann Roberts, maintained a steadfast commitment to the people and businesses of Chester County. A strong believer in community involvement, Ellen Ann is known throughout the region as a dedicated resident, and a believer in the people of Chester County.

Donna Coughey, the former CEO of Chester Valley Bancorp and today the CEO of Willow Financial Bank, has continued the commitment begun by Ms. Roberts. She also leads the development and growth of Willow Financial into the region's premier suburban-Philadelphia financial services provider. Across the organization, Willow Financial's employees dedicate their time and talent through a range of activities that make our neighborhoods and towns better places to live.

"It's important we provide the residents of Chester County with the wide range of products and focus on customer service they need and deserve from a community bank," says Ms. Coughey. "And we're committed to community support, through volunteerism and leadership. Willow Financial employees volunteer their time as members in chambers of commerce and

local business associations, including the Chester County Chamber of Business and Industry, Chester County Economic Development Council, and other organizations. Customers are our neighbors, and that understanding permeates everything we do as a bank and company."

Chester County's Employer of Choice

Willow Financial also serves the community as one of the area's premier employers. Employing over 400 people, the Bank offers ongoing training programs and excellent benefits that set Willow Financial apart as an Employer of Choice in the region.

"We believe that the Willow Financial Bank combination of community service, strong core product offerings, and reputation as a great place to work, sets it apart from other area banks," says Ms. Coughey.

"Our core values clearly reflect what we are all about - respect for every person; focus on the customer experience and be the best that you can be," says Colin Maropis, regional president. "By committing the bank to the community, and treating our employees with the same respect we do our clients and customers, we empower them to succeed in their positions. In my mind, that's most important benefit we can give them."

Promise to Customers – Exemplary Service

The Bank's customer promise is a simple one, "Always provide exemplary service by delivering an extraordinary banking experience that exceeds customer expectations."

"Exceeding our customers' expectations is first and foremost in providing them a superior banking experience," says Ms. Coughey.

Banking shouldn't be a hassle, and Willow Financial offers its customers the tools they expect – online banking, change machines in branches, expanded hours, and quality customer service. Branch employees know and recognize their customers, and offer them the personal service they deserve.

Willow Financial's commercial customers benefit from a team approach that helps customize banking and financial services for each unique situation. From Small Business Administration (SBA) loans to larger commercial loans, including commercial real estate and construction loans and lines of credit, we develop loan strategies that clear the way for quick settlement and rapid funding.

Our clients and customers in the process of accumulating or preserving wealth for their heirs, benefit from our Wealth Management practice, which offers integrated planning and high-touch services including Investment, Trust and Private Banking.

We invite you to find out what WillPower can do for you

Visit any local Willow Financial Bank branch location, visit our website at www.wfbonline.com, or contact us at 1-800-New Willow.

About Willow Financial Bank

Willow Financial is a $1.6 billion institution operating 28 conveniently located offices throughout Chester, Bucks, Montgomery and Philadelphia counties, with early morning, late evening and weekend hours.

Willow Financial Bancorp, Inc. is the holding company for Willow Financial Bank, a federally chartered savings bank, which is publicly traded on the NASDAQ Stock Market under the ticker WFBC. The Bank's headquarters are in Wayne, Pennsylvania.

For more information, please visit our website at www.wfbonline.com.

Genesis HealthCare℠

Genesis HealthCare Corporate Headquarters

Brandywine Center

Highgate at Paoli Pointe

Situated at the center of historic, downtown Kennett Square, Genesis HealthCare's award winning corporate headquarters, with its striking clock tower, is the keystone of Kennett's successful revitalization.

The 100,000 square foot, three story brick building with hand-made bricks, slate covered gables, extensive cornices, turrets, and other architectural flourishes was designed to fit into Kennett's historic streetscape.

Another major Genesis building--also sensitive to the architecture of Kennett Square-- is underway at the site of an old bank in the downtown area and will house the Company's information technology department. Genesis also transformed the former Clark Shoe factory building on Broad Street into offices.

Though the roots of parent company Genesis Health Ventures reach back to1985, Genesis HealthCare was created in 2003 through a spin-off of long-term care and rehabilitation therapy services divisions. Today, Genesis HealthCare is one of the nation's top skilled nursing, assisted living, and rehabilitation therapy providers. More than 35,600 Genesis employees provide round-the-clock care to more than 50,000 individuals annually in over 200 short and long-term care centers located in 12 eastern states.

In Kennett, over 600 Genesis employees provide back-office support for those skilled nursing, assisted living and rehab therapy locations.

For more information on Genesis, job opportunities, center locations or the latest company developments, visit www.genesishcc.com.

MEDecision

Since 1988, MEDecision has been a member of the Chester County community, growing from a start-up healthcare information technology company to a leader in collaborative care management. MEDecision's mission is simple— to improve the relationship between patients, payers and providers. From years of dedication and innovation, MEDecision provides leading solutions that meet what is now the most demanded market need in the healthcare industry—a way to collaborate.

Healthcare payers and providers recognize the need to become more collaborative in their approach to healthcare in order to improve the quality of care, reduce medical errors and increase operational efficiencies. MEDecision meets this need by providing collaborative care management solutions. Collaborative care management empowers payers, providers and patients with a common patient view of a person's health throughout the individual's continuum of care in order to foster better decisions. This improves the outcome and affordability of healthcare.

David St.Clair, the Founder and CEO of MEDecision, began his company in Chester County in 1988 and has grown it into one of the largest software employers in the Philadelphia region, ranking many times on the Philadelphia Business Journal's list of Top 25 Tech Employers. MEDecision is a member of the Philadelphia 100 Hall of Fame, having been named to the prestigious Philadelphia 100 list of fastest growing, privately-held companies five times or more. MEDecision has also ranked consecutively since 1998 on Healthcare Informatics's annual Top 100 listing of information technology companies serving the healthcare industry.

Accentuating the growth of the company and MEDecision's commitment to the community, in August 2004, the company moved its headquarters from Devon to the Chesterbrook Corporate Center, taking over 35,000 square feet of space. In August 2005, MEDecision celebrated more growth by expanding its operations into another building in Chesterbrook, occupying an additional 14,000 square feet. In August 2006, MEDecision expanded once again, adding another 40,000 square feet to the campus.

MEDecision is proud to play a role in leading the healthcare transformation to collaborative care management and is a proud member of the Chester County community.

MEDecision®
Collaborative Care Management

Wilkinson Builders

Charles Wilkinson and his family put their heart and soul into Wilkinson Builders, building each home with the same integrity as if it were being built for a member of their own family.

Wilkinson Builders was founded nearly three decades ago on a forward-thinking philosophy that continually searches for ways to improve... for new trends to set... for the latest state-of-the-art technology. Excelling in the art of home building,

Sales team members have extensive experience to assist homebuyers in the relocation process, including assistance throughout the mortgage process, consultation with design professionals as they personalize their new home, location of schools, the best places to shop... to eat... to unwind... and more!

Whether moving from another state or another country, buyers are offered a depth of knowledge in a wide range of areas.

Experience the quality that is integral to every Wilkinson home. Discover why hundreds of satisfied homeowners recommend Wilkinson Builders to their family and friends. Meet a builder with whom a handshake is a promise, and your satisfaction his highest accolade. Welcome home to Wilkinson Builders.

Wilkinson Builders is currently building new home communities in Chester County, Pennsylvania, and Kent and New

Wilkinson Builders has also learned more than a thing or two about customer service.

Wilkinson Builders' goal is to have every homebuyer receive an unparalleled level of customer service... in many communities, this is through constant communication with a personal Customer Liaison. New home buyers extol this creative approach, affirming that this unique process makes them feel as though their home is the only home being built.

Some team members are fluent in several languages; most are well experienced in the details of corporate relocation; all offer unequalled care and compassion during the process itself.

Wilkinson Builders also maintains a varied selection of Quick Settlement Homes available on a regular basis for buyers who need to settle quickly. Also available are corporate rental homes that can bridge the gap between Agreement of Sale and settlement, if necessary.

Castle Counties in Delaware. Current communities are varied, and include homes in lifestyle communities with clubhouses for adults 55 and over, (priced from the low $200's)... homes from $1.5 million... and everything in-between.

Information Centers and Model Homes are open daily from 12-5 and by appointment. For current quick settlement homes, maps, directions, and other information, please visit our website at WilkinsonBuilders.com.

The Devon Horse Show & Country Fair

Like many traditions in Chester County, the Devon Horse Show and Country Fair grew out of the customs of the countryside. In this case, it was the love of horses and leisurely carriage drives that prompted a group of local gentlemen to call a meeting in May of 1896 at an elegant hotel called the Devon Inn.

For years, the Inn had served as a summer retreat for Philadelphian businessmen and their families. But after the Pennsylvania Railroad built a railway through the area in 1830, more people traded the bustling city for rural Chester County. Here, they could enjoy leisurely weekend carriage drives as well as fox hunting and polo.

Not surprisingly, the discussion at the Inn revolved around the demand for horses and the need to showcase "the valuable thoroughbred breeding stock available...." In anticipation of its continued success, the men called the one-day event the "first annual" show. It was held on July 2, 1896 on the grounds of the Devon Polo Club, not far from the Inn.

The judges, who sat in a gazebo in the center of a grassy ring, must have had a relatively easy job. There were only thirty classes – none of them jumping classes – and the largest only had ten entries. Many also had titles that now seem quaint in their descriptions such as "Brood Mares with Foal at Foot" or "Stallions Suitable to get an All-purpose Horse."

From 1898 to 1900, the Devon Horse Show was held on the grounds of the Devon Inn where guests could watch the activities from its large rambling porches. However, for unexplained reasons, the show was not held from 1901 to 1909. When it was revived in 1910, it was touted as the Sixth Annual Exhibition and returned to the polo grounds. The show also took over the period allocated to the Philadelphia Horse Show which had closed, improvements were made to the polo grounds, including the construction of four wooded stands which contained Devon's famous "boxes," popular with families and parties bringing picnic lunches. Protected by canvas awnings, the boxes were linked by an extended boardwalk that served the ladies wearing long dresses or men in formal wear. There was even a bandstand for musicians.

Still, the show continued to bring together a colorful mixture of farmers and society types, horse breeders and country squires. One newspaper in 1907 described the scene: "The grandstand was filled, the track on one side lined with... innumerable rigs of all descriptions from the homely but useful hay wagon to the natty little dog cart...."

By 1917, Devon was the largest outdoor horse show in the United States. It was a founding member of the American Horse Shows Associations (AHSA), but it also continued to be a family-oriented social occasion. Indeed, show programs listed not only entries, owners, and advertisers, but also poems and songs about Devon. Reporters also routinely filled their news columns with descriptions of what people wore and who they were with, rather than the activities in the ring.

In 1919, the show officials designated the Bryn Mawr Hospital as the beneficiary of the show. They also added a Country Fair and incorporated the show's association so that shares could be sold to purchase the grounds, ensuring that the show had a permanent home. Under the leadership of Thomas W. Clark, who served as manager from 1919 to 1942, the Devon Horse Show and Country Fair, Inc., began to attract the nationally and internationally-known riders who participate today. It was Clark who introduced the tradition of naming days – "Children's Day," "Volunteer Day," "Marathon Day," for instance – and who oversaw the building of the main grand stand in 1923. Horses were also accommodated during this period with permanent stables. (Today, up to 900 horses can be housed on the grounds.)

The Great Depression of the 1930s did not seem to affect the show significantly. Indeed, it regularly drew 2,000 entries, and when the main ring was renovated and dedicated as the Wanamaker Oval in 1939, it was considered the largest show ring in the world. (The first lighted outdoor ring was added in 1941.)

The Second World War forced the cancellation of the show from 1943 to 1945, although organizers continued to reserve its show dates with the AHSA each year. They also celebrated its 50th anniversary when the show returned in 1946.

Only in the 1950s did competition from other shows spell trouble for the Devon Horse Show. William C. Hunneman, the show president, took charge however and confidently steered the show to greater heights. By the 1960s, the grounds had a new grandstand and a new ring, and jumper divisions such as the Grand Prix were added, securing its reputation as the place "Where Champions Meet."

In Devon's Centennial year in 1996, there were thirty-six divisions and 224 classes which drew World Cup Champion riders and Olympic medalists. As the oldest and largest outdoor multi-breed horse competition in the nation, Devon now appears on both society and sport pages. Yet it remains a place where families and friends can meet to enjoy the show or simply to stroll the grounds, which appears like a small lighted village at night, with its blue and white frame shops and its magically bright show rings.

Waterloo Gardens

Waterloo Gardens has been a Chester County tradition for more than 65 years. During that time, it has showcased the latest gardening and consumer trends while continuing to be family-owned and family-oriented.

In fact, Waterloo is now the largest garden center in the Tri-state area and one of the five most diversified garden centers in the country. It was also a unique place when it was first established in 1942 by James and Anna Paolini, the parents of the present CEO, Linda LeBoutillier. Its motto of the times was "Grower of Rare Plants."

Indeed, the Paolinis were so successful introducing a variety of plants to customers on the Main Line that in 1959, they purchased the present Exton property. Although it was initially used solely to grow nursery stock for the Devon branch, when the Exton area transformed from rural to suburban, a garden center was opened at the site in 1970.

When the Paolinis retired in 1972, they sold the business to their daughter Linda and her husband, Bo LeBoutillier. Diversification became their goal, and many rapid changes took place over the next decade. A large, beautiful greenhouse was built at the Devon location, and several different kinds of enterprises, including a gift and flower shop, a Christmas collectible shop, and a patio business were added to the company.

Although it has grown in size and scope, Waterloo's reputation as a source of new and unusual plants continues to be pre-eminent. In fact, part of the challenge

of introducing new concepts and plants is helping customers become knowledgeable about their investments in gardening. This is reflected in Waterloo's commitment to education.

The landscape division, for example, was established to meet the many requests from customers for their own "Waterloo garden."

Today, Waterloo Gardens has over 300 employees. Its educational services encompass workshops in horticulture and do-it-yourself decorating as well as environmental seminars and craft demonstrations. Waterloo even has "personal shoppers" to make gift purchasing easier.

Despite its growth, Waterloo continues to be "family-friendly." Indeed, Waterloo is now a destination shopping experience, drawing families year-round to participate in activities, events, and crafts.

This includes the annual Holiday Open House, drawing second and third generations of customers who want to be dazzled or inspired by the parade of designer-created Christmas trees which show-off Waterloo's unparalleled collection of ornaments and decorations.

Another tradition takes place the day after Thanksgiving when Santa illuminates

hundreds of thousands of lights from his fire engine. Hundreds of people attend this magical "Festival of Lights."

Waterloo also hosts a yearly ALS Hope Gala charity benefit, in memory of Bo LeBoutillier, who passed away in 2001 of Lou Gehrig's disease. The benefit takes place during the annual Flower Show & Garden Exposition.

What about the future? No doubt Waterloo Gardens will continue to "grow" as part of the ongoing effort to better serve its existing and ever-increasing customer base.

Morris Capital Advisors, Inc.

Morris Capital Advisors, Inc. is a dynamic and emerging money management company headquartered in Malvern, Chester County, offering a full range of investment services to its clients throughout the United States.

The company has earned national recognition for its investment results, including numerous Top Gun honors from Informa Investment Solutions of White Plains, New York, a nationally-recognized money manager data base that is respected throughout the financial industry. Also, the Wall Street Journal has ranked Morris Capital Advisors in the Large-Cap Core Category Kings section.

Since its founding in 1994, the company has utilized a defined investment philosophy for selected individual and institutional clients. Morris Capital Advisors, Inc. identifies companies with strong earnings and cash flow, the potential to grow over time, and a sound financial structure to support growth. Morris Capital Advisors then invests in companies whose share price is inexpensive relative to their valuation.

Morris Capital Advisors is an independent company that does its own research and bases its investment decisions on individual analysis of companies. "We use our own propriety evaluation model. We are not influenced by factors outside of our analytical process," Daniel A. Morris, company founding partner, said. "Our clients have direct access to our managers and we report to them in a manner that is clear and concise. We believe it is important for our clients to understand the way we manage their accounts."

One of the strengths of the company is the staff's wide range of expertise, which includes professionals with experience with major investment firms, banks, mutual funds and money management services.

Morris has more than 30 years in the investment profession. He started on his career after earning a degree from St. Vincent College in Pennsylvania and an M.S. in investments from Drexel University. As a portfolio manager at Wilmington Trust Company he managed more than $850 million and went on to be one of four founders of an institutional investment management company in Chadds Ford, Consistent Asset Management Company, where he managed more than $1 billion.

The key to being successful for a number of years, according to Morris, is offering expert money management with distinctive service for clients. "We value investments the same way that we value our business," Morris said. "We manage portfolios with a long-term investment horizon, using meaningful positions, diversified by economic sector. We believe that our analytical process will produce outstanding investment results for our clients over various market cycles."

"We want our clients to know that their investments are generating the best possible return, and that their client relationship is getting the attention it deserves," said John R. "Rusty" Giles, Director of Marketing and Client Services.

Morris Capital Advisors, Inc. is located at 15 Chester County Commons, Malvern, Pennsylvania. For more information, contact the company by calling 610 722-0900 or go to www.morriscapitaladvisors.com.

Bernardon Haber Holloway Architects PC

Chester County Justice Center

Abby Medical Center

Bernardon Haber Holloway Architects PC has been proudly serving Chester County since 1973. Led by the firm's four principals - Arthur Bernardon, AIA; Kerry Haber, AIA; William Holloway, AIA; and Neil Liebman, AIA - there are sixty staff members, including architects and interior designers, spread across three offices in Kennett Square and Downingtown, PA, and Wilmington, DE. Architecture, interior design, and land planning services are provided to a wide range of markets, including Corporate, Educational, Financial, Golf & Country Clubs, Health Care, Hospitality, Industrial, Religious, Residential, Retail, and Senior Care.

Our vision statement, "Forging Client Goals Into Valuable Assets," is exemplified by a commitment to listening. We strive to first understand and interpret a client's goals and then investigate the project constraints before beginning a design. There is nothing more rewarding than having a client confirm that we solved their problems. Often times, the built environment looks different than the client initially envisioned, because we have tailored the solution to meet project goals with value, efficiency, and interest to fit within its context.

Our commitment to being responsive and flexible in the way in which we provide our services is clear through our collaborative nature. Design reviews are held regularly so that anyone in the firm can offer advice, criticism, encouragement, or an alternate concept. A quality assurance program provides consistency in technical knowledge and carefully detailed construction drawings. The design process is geared toward providing the most successful design solution for each client.

Awards and recognition from local and regional community groups and professional associations acknowledge the role that we play in reinforcing the fabric of our local built environment. Bernardon Haber Holloway is proud of our involvement in Chester County and the active role of our staff members in organizations aimed at making Chester County a better place in which to live, work, and play.

Visit us at www.bernardon.com.

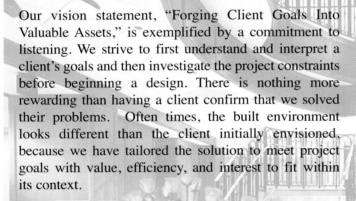

Genesis HealthCare Corporation

Genesis HealthCare Corporation

Kennett Area YMCA

Fieldstone Golf Club

Dansko   *Chester County Chamber of Business & Industry*

The Hankin Group

The Hankin Group has been developing real estate in Pennsylvania and New Jersey for more than 45 years. The company has completed projects from each specialty of construction and development including residential, retail, civic, office, laboratory and industrial.

In an effort to weave these elements into a complete community, The Hankin Group planned, developed and built Eagleview, a mixed use community of over 800 acres. Eagleview represents a concept for a new form of development, which encourages the placement of homes, shopping, recreation and business together in holistic ways that complement rather than disturb each other.

Eagleview is based on a lifestyle of "walkability," with sidewalks, jogging paths and greenways connecting and integrating the home, the market and the workplace. These components are unified by a town square replete with artwork, fountains, and space for gathering of people for holidays and special events. The Town Center, upon completion, will include retail and professional space, a civic building, luxury condominiums, and a medical building. The centerpiece is a two-acre park reminiscent of the commercial centers of New England villages and small southern towns of an earlier era.

Currently the Town Center consists of a retail building housing the Brickside Grille restaurant, La Vista Pizza, Salon di Domani, Sunnybrook Flowers, Wellington Square Book Shop and Wellington Square Curiosities. Other components of the Town Center include 18 Live Work units, Wellington Square Condominiums, the Lionville YMCA at Eagleview and the Potter Building – a four-story mid-rise affordable apartment building for seniors. All of this is within an evening stroll of 825 residential units and within a lunch hour walk for ultimately 5,000 thousand

people working in office buildings tucked away on intimate wooded sites, dramatic hillside locations, or along the landscaped boulevards. The Hankin Group strives to reverse the modern trends of suburban sprawl and lengthy commutes while still providing high quality housing and maintaining affordability and aesthetic beauty.

As new concepts for creating better communities are proven successful in Eagleview, they are recreated and improved for other locations. Weatherstone, a new community of 273 single family

and town home residences gracefully compliments the area's pastoral beauty with its 195 acres of open space, while its neo-traditional neighborhood design perfectly integrates home and community life. Weatherstone is also the home of the Henrietta Hankin branch of the Chester County Library.

The Hankin Group believes that future growth and development in Chester County can be achieved in partnership with local government and that the existing natural beauty can be preserved.

Vanguard

Vanguard's business philosophy and guiding principles are based on the simple but revolutionary idea that mutual funds should be managed in the sole interest of their shareholders. Unlike many investment firms that are privately held or publicly traded, Vanguard is client-owned.

be compromised. Vanguard pioneered an educational, plain-talk approach to investor communications. These actions, and many others, were motivated by our commitment to delivering consistent performance and outstanding service at the lowest possible cost.

perspectives, knowing that it makes us a better, stronger company.

Vanguard offers excellent career opportunities in financial, technical, IT, client service, and other disciplines. All employees are eligible for a complete Total Rewards benefits package that includes competitive and comprehensive paid time off, medical, vision, prescription, and dental coverage; flexible spending accounts; life insurance; legal services; 401(k) and profit-sharing; and tuition reimbursement. Employees also enjoy work-life balance initiatives, including flexible schedules and a number of on-site, convenience services; extensive training and development; on-campus fitness facilities; scholarships; and employee discount programs.

Helping our investors achieve their goals is literally the company's sole reason for existence. With no other parties to answer to, and, therefore, no conflicting loyalties, Vanguard makes every business decision with only its clients' needs in mind.

For example, offering an index mutual fund to individual investors was unheard of when Vanguard did it in 1976; today indexing is a heralded investing approach. Because of the low costs and tax efficiency that indexing offers, investors can have more of their money working for them. We were one of the first mutual fund firms to eliminate sales loads, and to close funds when current shareholders' interests could

Vanguard was launched in 1975, but our heritage extends back to 1929 with the inception of Wellington™ Fund, one of the longest-operating funds of any kind. Today, Vanguard is a world-class provider of a complete line of financial products and services, with total assets of more than $980 billion. We employ a diverse workforce of more than 11,000 talented individuals in our three U.S. locations – Malvern, PA, Scottsdale, AZ, and Charlotte, NC – and in our offices in Europe, Japan, and Australia. Diversity is a core value, fully supported at every level of the company. We actively foster an environment enriched by different

Community involvement is inherent in Vanguard's culture. Employees have pledged more than $2 million annually to the United Way, and contributions rise each year. Our Community Volunteers program maintains partnerships with an array of nonprofit organizations. And through regular drives, employees donate food, blood, books, holiday gifts, computers, clothing, tax-filing assistance, and even cell phones to various organizations.

Vanguard has been recognized locally and nationally as an employer of choice. In January 2006, FORTUNE magazine named Vanguard - for the fifth time in six years - one of the "100 Best Companies to Work For." In September 2004, AARP named Vanguard one of the "Best Companies for Workers over 50." Vanguard has also received accolades from *Computerworld* magazine (June 2006), *Essence* magazine (May 2005), *Training* magazine (2006), *The Black Collegian* magazine (2005), and *Information Week* (September 2004).

To learn more about Vanguard and available career opportunities, please visit us at www.vanguard.com.

Jackson Cross Partners

YOUR REAL ESTATE PARTNERS AT EVERY POINT OF INTERSECTION

There are many critical points in the life cycle of owning or occupying a property. The financial and operational impact of decisions made at those critical points can deeply affect the success of an enterprise. That's why Jackson Cross Partners has developed a comprehensive service platform that provides clear vision at every point of intersection.

• Knowledge Assembly

Because making proactive and informed decisions regarding commercial real estate cannot be done without accurate and timely information, Jackson Cross has developed a process-centered approach to information gathering and management that fully enhances strategic real estate decision-making, as a key element to your overall business plan.

• Planning & Analysis

At Jackson Cross, our artful application of technology allows us to bring a different perspective – a critical and analytical view, and creative solutions to the challenges presented in each project, while helping you evaluate the optimal strategy going forward.

• Project Execution

Once a plan is implemented, it is critical to provide the skills, resources and single point-of-control to ensure successful execution. Our market specialization, resources and experience provide the deal-making skills and business savvy to deliver consistently exceptional results.

• Continuing Management

Jackson Cross is committed to your success every day – not just the day the

deal is done. The Jackson Cross Way creates a partnership, which allows us to regularly consult with you so we can proactively identify opportunities to adjust your real estate plan to changing business demands.

MARKETS SERVED

Jackson Cross Partners offers comprehensive market coverage throughout the Metropolitan Philadelphia area. With offices in Pennsylvania, Delaware and New Jersey, as well as strategic partnerships throughout the world, we can service large and small corporations, and real estate investors and developers – wherever their needs may arise. Our process-centered approach is fully exportable to other markets and we have regularly directed projects for clients in cities throughout North America and Europe. As the Philadelphia partner of ONCOR International, we can provide local expertise and market intelligence in over 200 markets worldwide.

In addition, our partnership with NorthMarq Capital, one of the largest commercial mortgage bankers in the United States, provides our clients with ready access to equity and debt financing from premier funding sources, for projects large and small.

JACKSON CROSS PARTNERS COMMERCIAL REAL ESTATE SERVICES

Our Guiding Principles

RESPECT EACH INDIVIDUAL WE ENCOUNTER.

DISTINGUISH OURSELVES BY THE *QUALITY* OF OUR WORK.

UPHOLD OUR REPUTATION FOR *INTEGRITY*.

For more information contact us at:
www.jacksoncross.com

Or call:

King of Prussia	610-265-7700
Philadelphia	215-564-2720
Delaware	302-792-1301
New Jersey	856-467-8055

JACKSON CROSS
PARTNERS ℅
ONCOR INTERNATIONAL

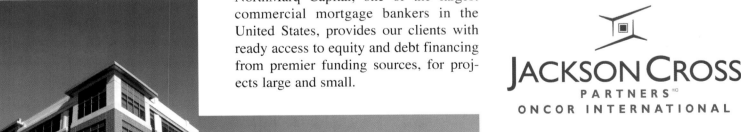

Longwood Gardens

Longwood Gardens if one of the horticultural treasures of America. Recalling the great pleasure gardens of Europe, Longwood exemplifies a twentieth-century approach to classic Old World traditions.

The gardens were once the country home of Pierre S. du Pont (1870-1954), an industrial wizard and financier extraordinaire. He turned the DuPont Chemical Company into a corporate empire and used his personal fortune to transform Longwood into a veritable paradise of plants and flowers.

The actual story of Longwood begins more than 200 years before du Pont's involvement. In 1700, an English Quaker named George Peirce purchased 402 acres of the present property from William Penn's commissioners. Although the property was primarily a farm, it became a renowned arboretum under Peirce's great-grandsons, Joshua and Samuel Peirce.

Working together, the brothers began building their arboretum in 1798, at times traveling by horseback as far as the Catskill Mountains of New York and south to Maryland's cypress swamps to obtain new plants. They also collected species closer to home, including the Kentucky coffee tree and cucumber magnolia, both natives of western Pennsylvania.

By the mid 1800's, the arboretum was known as Peirce's Park and was open for parties and picnics. Although the groves of native, European, and Asian trees remained key attractions, the property and its ponds were carefully developed into a pleasure ground, in keeping with the public parks movement then sweeping the country.

By 1897, the park involved another generation of the Peirce family, but they had little interest in horticulture and the property soon fell into disrepair. After 200 years of family ownership, the property was put up for sale and resold several times. In 1906, Pierre du Pont, then 36, came to the rescue of Peirce's Park whose century-old trees were about to be cut down and milled for lumber. Although du Pont later called his purchase and "attack of insanity," it was more than a whim. He saw the property as an ideal setting for a country retreat and profitable farm.

Renaming the property "Longwood" du Pont began an ambitious project that spanned decades and indulged his increasing interest in grand, European-style horticulture and whimsy. In 1907, for instance, he laid out Longwood's first true Flower Garden Walk where he experimented with what he called an "old-fashioned" influence, with nostalgic cottage-style garden flowers, exuberant shrubs, rose-laden trellises, and rustic benches. There was even a picturesque arbor, a birdbath, and a shiny "gazing ball."

Du Pont was so pleased with the springtime effect that he hosted the first of many lavish garden parties in June, 1909. They were held almost annually from 1931 until 1940 and were the highlight of the Wilmington social season as well as the inspiration for many ongoing garden improvements.

Following a visit to Italy in 1913, du Pont built an outdoor theater on the site of the original Peirce barn. It featured a 68-foot-wide stage with hemlock trees as stage wings and was a great success with du Pont's friends at its debut in June, 1914. Within a year, du Pont began the expansion of the old Peirce family home, adding Longwood's first conservatory, now part of an historical exhibit. It was completed in time to celebrate his marriage to a woman who shared his love of horticulture, Alice Belin.

A much larger conservatory opened nearby in 1921. Its elegant arched windows and classic form created a spectacular setting for winter parties and for growing du Pont's favorite plants: roses and azaleas and fruit of all kinds including oranges, figs, nectarines, peaches, and pineapples. Du Pont added an elegant music room to the conservatory in 1923; a huge azalea house in 1928; and a resplendent ballroom, complete with a pink etched-glass ceiling, crystal chandeliers, and a walnut parquet floor by 1929. A 10,010-pipe organ was the centerpiece of the room.

Du Pont in later years began to spend more of his time on philanthropic and personal interests, especially on his gardens. In 1925, for instance, he added a magnificent Italian Water Garden featuring 600 fountain jets. The last major construction project – Longwood's Main Fountain Garden – was launched in 1928 and was nearly eight years in development. It not only rivaled the fountains du Pont had seen thirty-five years earlier at the World's Fair in Chicago, it was considered an engineering feat of its day. Its recirculating system of eighteen pumps still propels 10,000 gallons of water a minute to heights as high as 130 feet through 380 gushing spouts. The fountains can be illuminated at night in all colors of the rainbow.

As early as 1941, du Pont began to consider the eventual fate of the property after his death and incorporated the Longwood farm. In 1937, the Longwood Foundation was created to handle du Pont's charitable donations, and in 1946, the government gave approval for the Foundation to operate Longwood "for the sole use of the public...." Thus, when du Pont died in 1954, at the age of 84, he left Longwood with a well-established horticultural tradition and a generous endowment.

Today, Longwood is one of the world's most renowned public gardens. Its horticultural displays are complemented by Longwood's educational programs, theater productions, and seasonal festivals as well as hundreds of annual activities. All serve in their way to continue du Pont's legacy to delight new guests and to keep old friends returning to Longwood time and time again.

Chester County Historical Society

Founded in 1893, the Chester County Historical Society is a not-for-profit educational institution that promotes an understanding of the history of Chester County and southeastern Pennsylvania. The Historical Society is unique; it is the only organization dedicated to preserving the heritage of the entire county.

The heart of the institution is its collections, which provide the basis for its award-winning exhibitions. The museum houses more than 70,000 objects. These range from what many people think of when they hear "museum" – fine art and antiques – to items that speak of everyday life. The Historical Society not only owns a Queen Anne desk made by local cabinet-maker Joel Bayly in 1732 and artworks by Horace Pippin, it also has a 1949 Ironrite automatic ironer used by a local family until 1989.

The Historical Society's library holds an extensive collection of family and local history resources. Like the museum collection, these tell the history of a wide range of people, places, and events. Manuscripts reflect events as monumental as the American Revolution or as individual as holding a hummingbird in one's hand. The first story is told in the "Depredations Book," a listing of items plundered by British troops in 1777. The second is found in an 1844 account book of Joseph Hawley: "I caught a humming-bird as smart as it was, after I viewed it, it cried so I let it go. And I was this fall 72 years old."

The newspaper clipping collection was described in a national genealogical journal as "one of the state's best." The photo archives has over 80,000 images, from daguerreotypes – including a rare image of a young Frederick Douglass – to color prints and digital images. The Historical Society, in cooperation with the County of Chester, administers the County Archives, which houses over 300 years of county government records, making it one of the most complete in Pennsylvania.

The Historical Society is, however, more than its collections. The education staff provides interactive and hands-on experiences for students to engage them in the study of the community's past. Program offerings include on-site field trips, such as walking tours of West Chester; outreach activities include traveling trunks of reproduction artifacts, which contain lessons on the American Revolution, women's history, and other subjects. The staff also travels to schools to offer programs about the Underground Railroad and other topics. Programming for adults is another aspect of the Historical Society; the annual Antiques Show, workshops on family history, and talks by local authors are just some of the regular offerings. The Historical Society also has a museum shop, which offers local crafts, books, and other items that relate to the region's past.

In addition to the library and museum, the Historical Society features classrooms and an auditorium, which may be rented for events and community programs. Membership provides free admission for research or a visit to the museum galleries, as well as an opportunity to attend special programs.

The Historical Society is located at 225 North High Street in West Chester. Please call 610-692-4800 or visit www.chestercohistorical.org to find out about current exhibitions, programming, membership and more.

The Chester County Courthouse in West Chester.

Chester County Scenes

◀ ◀ ◀ ◀ **Covered bridge at Valley Forge**
◀ ◀ ◀ **Farm on Creek Road**
◀ ◀ **Foggy sunrise in cattle country**
◀ **Autumn patterns**
Chester County horse farm ▶

We would like to thank the following groups and individuals for their cooperation in assisting us in our research or granting access to their properties.

The Chester County Historical Society
The Chester County Parks and Recreation Department
Brandywine Battlefield Park
The Brandywine Conservancy and River Museum
The Devon Horse Show and Country Fair, Inc.
The French & Pickering Creeks Conservation Trust, Inc.
Historic Yellow Springs, Inc.
Longwood Gardens
Radnor Hunt Club